The Devout Life

THE DEVOUT LIFE

William Law's Understanding of Divine Love

Edited and introduced by
Martin Israel and Neil Broadbent

Continuum
London and New York

CONTINUUM
The Tower Building, 11 York Road, London SE1 7NX
370 Lexington Avenue, New York, NY 10017-6503

www.continuumbooks.com

First published 2001

British Library Cataloguing-in-Publication Data
A catalogue record for this book is available from the British Library.

ISBN 0 264 67532 0

Typeset by YHT Ltd, London
Printed and bound in Great Britain by Biddles Ltd, Guildford and King's Lynn

Contents

Preface

This book shows the way of growth of a man who was schooled in a puritanical way of thought, but through the influence of the mystical tradition emerged from a shell of exclusiveness to an over-arching love and comprehensiveness. It indicates both the limitations of much conventional religion and a way in which it could move beyond sheer dogma to a universal understanding of spirituality.

'Would you know who is the greatest saint in the world: It is not he who prays most or fasts most, it is not he who gives most alms or is most eminent for temperance, chastity or justice; but it is he who is always thankful to God, who wills everything that God wills, who receives everything as an instance of God's goodness and has a heart always ready to praise God for it.'[1]

'There is nothing that makes us love a man so much as praying for him.'[2]

In the above and subsequent excerpts from the writings of the Reverend William Law occasional, slight adjustments to punctuation and grammar have been made to assist the modern reader. Care has been taken to ensure Law's meaning is unaltered.

Biblical passages at the bottom of each page show the manner in which Law's work relates to Holy Scripture.

Acknowledgements

The Revd Robert Llewelyn for his encouragement to produce this book and graciously allowing us to use his previous work. Dr Petà Dunston of the Divinity School Library, Cambridge for her generous assistance over several years in tracking down out-of-print materials.

All Scripture references are taken from the Revised English Bible unless otherwise stated.

PART ONE

Introductory Essays

Loving the Hell Out of Us

It seems paradoxical that the God whom humanity worships as a beneficent Creator so often fills his creatures with confusion.

Our view of God tends to be formed at a very early age: an irrelevant 'God of our ancestors', a tyrant or 'there is no such being.' In Christian society, God in Christ may be seen to act rather as Superman, zooming into conflict and trouble, and mightily saving 'the good guys' from great perils. A gentler image involves an elderly, white-bearded gentleman sitting on a cloud, surrounded by young, winged creatures with human faces understood to be angels.

To state the obvious, parents and grandparents can only pass on what they believe and know. Teachers can only teach and preachers only preach what has been handed on to them by study and experience. The innocence of a very young child is all too quickly lost through a series of necessary, and inevitably bruising, battles of will with parents, relatives and school friends. As a polite version of Philip Larkin's poem says:

'They muck you up, your mum and dad.
They may not mean to, but they do.
They fill you with the faults they had
And add some extra, just for you.'[1]

For not a few children, being loved may mean knuckling under whatever is the will of the moment of a responsible adult. The small child looks up and sees inconsistent expressions of power.

Unsurprisingly, God becomes seen as a capricious, omnipotent demander of acceptable behaviour. Blessed are they who have always known God as love.

The world-class exponents of religion, known as the mystics, are the individuals to whom God has granted a very deep experience of his total love for them and all creation. Whilst reading from the German Lutheran mystic Jacob Boehme, the zealous William Law was overwhelmed by an inner conviction that God was, and is, Love; all Love, entire absolute Love: nothing but pure, total Love.

What if this is true; that the ultimate power in the universe is not whimsical, does not change its mind and does not browbeat or require a fight? What if 'God is Love,' and he asks only that one lives in and from his perfect love? This would certainly tie in well with the teaching of Jesus that one must 'love the Lord your God with all your heart, with all your soul, with all your mind and with all your strength.' And 'You must love your neighbour as yourself.'[2] The bottom line, as Jesus knew well, is that love is the quintessential source for self-acceptance, self-esteem and caring awareness of our neighbours' circumstances.

It's one thing to be told how to behave and quite another to achieve it. If God is only perfect love and he is all-powerful why is it that our relationships are not more fully loving also? Psychotherapists can shed light on the hidden sources of repressed distresses that lead to damaging behaviour, but whether or not such materials are resolved and integrated is another matter. Our ability to be open to perfect, heavenly love is curtailed by our own unconscious processes, established when we were very young children.

In the first year of life, the baby has all sorts of needs of which the most important are security and survival. Where these are sufficiently met at the time the baby feels them, its senses of security and self-esteem are fostered and encouraged. On occasions when mum, or a prime carer, is not able instantly to gratify the infant, then something akin to a panic, due to escalating strong feelings, emerges. This eventually becomes too much and explodes on to the surroundings, or, as other people will, by and large, put up with only so many explosions, this emotional turmoil is swallowed up deep inside – as if it had been annihilated. Awareness of the pain of unfulfilled needs is blotted out and repressed into the unconscious. The need has not gone away and our body somehow still remembers the event. Our emotional life is greatly affected – but we are no longer aware of this.

The one-year-old's awareness and needs are growing steadily. Now its needs include esteem, affection and pleasure. Only on some occasions can such urgent demands be fully met. Sometimes the child settles for 'good enough'. Those times when great urges and needs are not met create huge confusion for the toddler. As time goes by and the youngster learns more and more, so new needs become very important: for group acceptance, for power, and control to some degree in our daily lives.

All this is developing before the child can speak much or begin to reason and think clearly. For those times in which it has felt thwarted, it invents strategies to try to increase the occasions when its desires are satisfied. Thomas Keating calls these strategies 'emotional programmes for happiness'.[3] They are formulated at stages prior to clear thinking and reasoning, so that by the age of, say, seven- to ten-years-old the child's reasoning skills are used to confirm and bolster these unconscious strategies.

With growing age arises more and more responsibility, so for many people these 'emotional programmes for happiness' remain unconsidered. Preferences, prejudices, irrational fears, anxieties and life-coping strategies are ensconced within us. The focus of our activities is largely outwards, so that before we know it we come to the point of saying, 'I am as I am, warts and all; take me or leave me.' One's defences against further large rejections are taken to be OK. 'I won't tread on your toes if you don't tread on mine.' So groups grow up with the unspoken, unwritten agenda of 'Don't rock the boat,' 'Keep to the party line if you know what is good for you.' As Menzies wrote in 1970, large institutions may function at a deep level as social systems organized to keep at bay individual and corporate anxieties.[4]

This lack of awareness or consciousness is a source of troubles great and small for many years to come. Retired folk can still be at the mercy of unreconciled emotional pains from early life.

The wise person does not look to improve their therapeutic skills, unless such is their work. Rather they practise turning this material over to the Saviour through prayer.

This individual and collective unawareness is the basis of the theological word *sin*. Sin is something far more subtle than inappropriate sexual activity – it is living in a less than perfectly (divinely) loving manner with our selves, our neighbours, the world and the Creator. Sin is running on less than 100 per cent divine fuel. It is living by the human spirit rather than the Holy Spirit. Divinization is sidelined.

We know from Holy Scripture that 'perfect love banishes fear.'[5] Love can be defined, in the words of Lord Coggan, one-time Archbishop of Canterbury, as 'the set of the will towards the eternal well-being of the beloved'. Growing in Christian faith therefore is growth in love and out of fear, and such spiritual growth has much to do with the exercise of human will.

Simply deciding that one *will* not gossip behind another's back, spread knowledge that can drag someone down or brag of one's own achievements rarely works for long. The reason is that one's energies tend to be focused negatively on what one wants to avoid, and such concentration is draining. It is far better to focus on the positive.

Hence the need to cherish the thought that God, absolute love, loves each and every soul absolutely. God completely and totally cherishes us moment by moment. 'At all times and in all places' it is right for us to give God thanks and praise, as the rite for Holy Communion has it, because at all times and in all circumstances he loves us infinitely and eternally.

All the great mystics have experienced overwhelming divine love in their lives, and possibly none more so in England than the Reverend William Law. His youthful and rigoristic attitudes came, in time, to melt away. His fearful insistence in making every endeavour to 'be ye perfect as your heavenly father is perfect' was washed away in a tide of delight and praise when a far greater knowledge of God was granted him.

This better understanding was not instantaneous. We know Law spent nine years learning High Dutch in order to be able to translate Jacob Boehme's work into English. The actual texts that William Law studied can be read today in the County Records Office at Wootton Hall, Northampton, on application to the duty archivist.

Julian of Norwich spent twenty years reflecting upon the true meaning of the revelations granted to her. We may take it then that true spiritual growth is a very slow process.

Deepening knowledge of the God who is always perfectly loving towards us enables us gradually, but more completely as the years roll by, to let go of fears – fears of others, fear of God and fears in or of our own selves.

In William Law's day it was accepted in church circles that there was only one God, one Saviour, and one humanity; that all mankind was considered as one in its collective humanity. There was one Adam, representing the fall of mankind, and only one 'second Adam', Jesus, who shows the way for the return of this one humanity back to at-one-ment with the Divine. The popular focusing on Jesus by Christians makes sense when Jesus is seen as the representative man, standing for any and all humanity.

Perfect love perfectly allows the beloved to think and do as they choose. And to choose to cling to anything like the rich young man of Mark's gospel[6] and Mary Magdalene of John's[7] is to choose to remain closed to the sacrament of the present moment. If, like Peter who denied knowing Jesus on three occasions after his betrayal,[8] we insist on living out old patterns of understanding and relating, we close ourselves up in a state of mind that can only bring failings.

This is indeed what the first part on 'God and humanity' shows us.

The second, and largest, section is the heart of the book. It describes the goal of Christian life as 'doing the will of God' and shows how it may be, and why it frequently is not, achieved.

In the many forms of religion based upon fear – fundamentalisms of any kind – the participants are easily persuaded to cast out of themselves and project on to other people all the failings which they carry within themselves. According to one's upbringing there may be much of which one wishes to be rid, and psychological mechanisms of scapegoating and demonizing come into play. This is not the divine solution: it is a very human expression of panic, haste and, to some degree, fear. 'Which is only saying that all the powers and properties of [human] nature are a misery to themselves, [and] can only work in disquiet and anger, until the birth of the Son of God brings them under the dominion and power of the spirit of love.'[9]

Discovering that we can never take a holiday from our own selves or from relating to creation and Creator, it slowly dawns on us that the events of our everyday lives are the very real ingredients with which we fashion our spiritual lives. The religious person sees life's daily events as opportunities for spiritual growth and development. Outwardly the day brings what it will; the way in which one inwardly chooses to respond to each moment *is* spiritual exercise.

Having established the nature of God and our fallen but not

forsaken relationship with him, it becomes apparent that the inner battle, turmoil, spiritual war lies between doing things our way or in accordance with perfect love, the Christ way. The struggle then is to rely less on the things of this life alone and more on the things that resonate with the eternal; a struggle between personal and corporate human desires (hubris) and prayer.

It is not only Adam and Eve who chose to eat from the wrong tree of knowledge. Daily we promote hubris and chaos unless we are in the habit of re-turning, primarily in our thoughts – for 'As a man thinks in his heart so he is'[10] – but also in our actions to the one eternal source of all beauty, truth and goodness. 'We are strangers to heaven and without God in the world, for this reason only, that we are void of that spirit of prayer which alone can unite, and never fails to unite us with the one only Good, and to open heaven and the kingdom of God within us.'[11]

Guarding and cherishing our thoughts, and the examining of them, is a requisite part of spiritual progress. The reason for this is because thinking and free will are eternal. That which thinks and wills in the soul is that very same unbeginning breath which thought and willed in God. So 'the state of our will makes the state of our life.'[12] 'This is the purity and perfection of life that we pray for in the Lord's Prayer, that God's kingdom may come and his will be done in us as it is in heaven.'[13] And the reason why we are not more loving, more holy and wholesome than we presently are is because we wish and will for more than one thing. 'The multiplicity of wills is the very essence of fallen nature, and all its evil, misery and separation from God lies in it.'[14]

Our thoughts easily lead us astray; to concentrate on things that puff us up with vainglory or pride, with anger, greed, lust or self-pity. Some people desire constantly to feel or believe they are superior, such may be the strength of their insecurities. On the other hand, to think kind and loving thoughts of peace, health and harmony about another person or group is a form of praying for them, so close is the link between thought and prayer.

Learning new ways in the spiritual life often entails relinquishing old habits of thinking[15] and relating. Such a change in direction is the basis of *metanoia* (literally, 'a change of mind') – or repentance. Hence a true relationship with Almighty love always includes a deepening awareness of one's folly, stupidity or sin, which is culpable separation from God.

These are like two sides of a single coin: they are inseparable. Yet this need not cause us to despair, but rather continually point us back to the only source of true happiness and joy. Sunbathing – bathing in the light of the Son of God – is essential. So the myth (which is a spiritually true story) goes: God created humanity on the sixth day, and on the seventh he rested. Humanity's first task then was to rest and delight in all that God had made.[16]

Indeed, it is right first to relax, let go and trust in the ever-present goodness of God, and then align oneself by an act of will with the one whose law is love in perfect freedom and who seeks our freely offered cooperation. Hurrying is often a sign of personal preoccupation rather than waiting upon the Lord. With constancy on God's part, for he has no need to change, any inconsistencies and inconstancy in one's relationship with the Divine must be on our side.

Whilst we need air for every breath in this life, still more important is prayer that we need for every breath in this life and the next. Prayer is to the soul as air is to the body, revealing that 'everyone's life is a continual state of prayer.' [17]

Prayer predisposes us to learn the deepest lesson of the human heart: that divine light ever shines in human darkness. Spiritual growth is about immersing ourselves in a spirit of prayer which leads us into the way of divine knowledge, ultimately incorporating our being into the Spirit of love.[18]

We know the shape of a human life totally dedicated to God. Great trials in wildernesses of various kinds precede and succeed celebratory moments, for example, just like Jesus' entry into Jerusalem.[19]

A great personal or family calamity may turn out to be the gateway to deeper comprehension of human weakness and God's strong compassion. A very real inability to save ourselves from the consequences of human folly or natural disaster can become the springboard from whence we may leap into the divine lap and allow the Almighty to encompass us with his everlasting arms.

Trials and devastations, obviously permitted by the Almighty, lead us by degrees from pride to humility and from anger to prayer; the work of the Holy Spirit is one of softening judgements into discernments. Law's words about anger are given as an example of the complex ways in which we confound and confuse ourselves.

When we see a long dark shadow in front of us, it is not because the sun has turned black, rather that we have turned our back upon it. 'It is much more possible for the sun to give out darkness than for God to do or be, or give out anything but blessing or goodness,' wrote Law.[20]

Along the way, much will need to be abandoned. As well as multitudes of fears – many masquerading as indignations, prides or 'must-have essentials' of daily life – attitudes need to be relinquished. Old understandings are jettisoned to allow room for the presence of the Lord, the Holy One, to grow in our hearts and minds, bodies and souls. This giving up, or forsaking, is the kind Jesus spoke of, 'Anyone who has left brothers or sisters, or father, or mother, or children, for the sake of my name will be repaid many times over, and gain eternal life.'[21]

We have seen earlier in this essay how false, but utterly understandable 'programmes for emotional happiness' are generated at a very young age, and how fears lie at the bottom of such compulsive powers within us. One comes to discover that the most common cause of failing to live in harmony and perfect love is the way we react to strong feelings which at times seem to overwhelm us from outside but which in reality are merely released from deep within us.

Our varied responses to our selves and to others are frequently automatic and based upon personal prejudices, preferences and fears; given early childhood it could hardly be otherwise. But when we become adult we are bidden to put away childish attitudes and see things more clearly. To do this, we need among other things to polish the mirror of our souls by a disciplined and regular practice of the means of our faith: prayer, meditation, silence and contemplation, public worship, Bible reading and reception of the sacraments. Penitence – even going to a priest or minister to make an act of confession – is a much neglected yet powerful tool for growing in holiness and returning to the divine.

The journey to the promised land may entail many years in the wilderness of incomprehension and struggle, until we learn that the ways of the Lord will seem strange whilst we live with delusions of personal ability or strength. What may have been thought large achievements come to be counted as dross, and vice versa, for 'when I am weak [in self-reliance], then I am strong [in Christ].'[22]

Law's writings may seem very deep, abstract and learned but there is nothing more practical than a good theory – or, in this case, theology. All the ways of God to man are ways of love, and desirous of increasing love throughout creation. 'God is the one who loves the hell out of us.'[23] William Law shows us that 'True faith is coming to Jesus Christ to be saved and delivered from a sinful nature, as the Canaanitish woman came to him and would not be denied.'[24]

This, in a nutshell, is Law's answer to the question, 'How do we follow Jesus?' To want – or even to want to want – what God wills for us in our lives, therein lies the path to wholeness and holiness.

The theory can be understood long before it is put into practice; much as a depressed person after ten years of psychotherapy may be able to explain everything about their depression and still not move beyond it. So it is that for many folk momentous beginnings – for example, 'Here is the stuff of which fairy tales are made; the prince and princess on their wedding day'[25] – so often move through depression, redundancy, divorce or death into a deeper, truer and simpler relationship with all those around them.

Growth in holiness, becoming more like Jesus, entails more than being seen with the right people, or at the right time saying acceptable words. Do we endeavour to see each moment for what it is, something to which we may respond charitably? Or as something which is hindering our own hidden, urgent agendas – suitably rationalized and sanitized for public exposure?

Divinization proceeds by regularly pausing before responding[26] throughout each day. This encourages more awareness of a reality far stronger than our strongest passions: the compassion of the divine life. 'Be still and know that I am God,' as the psalmist wrote.[27]

This section of the book describes the movements between pride and humility, and how the former is to be abandoned and the second sought. Pulling no punches, pride is seen as hell and heaven as humility.

God's ways with humanity are described in the Holy Scriptures. Regular reading and reflection upon them, remembering that the psalms were Jesus' own prayer book, leads us to the awareness that 'there is but one salvation for all mankind, and that is the life of God in the soul.' [28]

Worship, prayer, service to others and sacraments all draw us onwards in ever greater expansions of consciousness towards that time when we can look upon ourselves or another person, see and understand them for who they are, and assist them on their journey towards fulfilment in divine love.

Anything less we must lift high to the enduring power of perfect love at the place of the skull that is called Golgotha.

Love flourishes only where self is offered up, and sacrifice is made for the benefit, the blessing of others. All else partakes of the endlessly varied forms of self-exaltation which Law appropriately names the antichrist.

The third and final section goes over the same ground as the first two. Repetition is essential in life: one does not usually, by choice, eat only one meal a day, assure loved ones that they are loved but once a year, or take only one breath to last each minute. So the essentials need to be constantly affirmed.

There is a deepening of earlier points and an expansion into considerations of the Holy Trinity, of heaven and hell and of universal redemption.

Salvation is not in what style of doctrine we believe but in how we conduct our relationships. Doctrine arises from deep reflection upon experience. Daily examination of conscience will deepen our awareness that the work of the Spirit is within; the fruits will be manifested outwardly, but the work is interior. Hence there is the need for a growing and deepening silence, the need to still a chattering mind and rein in curiosity over the state of other people's lives.

As our outward energies slow down and fail, so our inner awareness and journeyings may deepen. For some the adventure of man living on the moon or travelling to see whether there is life on Mars may seem of ultimate significance. To a sensitive soul these can be seen as outward projections of the inner search to discover the biblical kingdom of God within oneself; an adventure that requires every bit as much study, training and discipline.

The last section therefore consists of the consequences of improved reflection and prayer: greater awareness – 'sensibility' is the word Law uses – of the Holy Trinity, of heaven, hell and the happiness of doing only what God wills. We discover the futility of pretending to a greater degree of holiness or perfection than we have. We learn that whether we are praised or condemned we are not to dwell on either, but refocus our desires upon the Lord, seeking only what he wills, for such is our true meat and drink.[29]

The practice of paying silent attention to everyday events in a spirit of loving prayer for all parties brings salvation nearer to all involved. Newness of life is to be found in response to the knocking of Christ upon the door of our heart in the present moment's circumstances.

Let us consider now William Law's place in Christian mysticism.

William Law's place in Christian Mysticism

The historical background

The religious scene had been quite violent in seventeenth-century England. After Elizabeth Tudor had died without issue the throne passed into the House of Stuart. James I's period of supremacy was comparatively peaceful, but his successor, Charles I, was embroiled in increasing controversy with the extremely Protestant Puritans.

These were led by Oliver Cromwell, who, in the Civil War that began in 1642, assumed power and worked towards the deposition of Charles I. This was achieved in 1649, when the king was executed. Cromwell, who then became the ruler of the country, assumed the title of 'Lord Protector' in 1653. The country was called a 'Commonwealth'.

Though an excellent military commander (with a notorious hatred of Irish Roman Catholics) and a moderate Puritan ruler, he was never popular with the people and when he died in 1658 he was replaced, after a two-year hiatus, by a scion of the House of Stuart. This was Charles II, who assumed office in 1660.

Charles II's rule lasted until 1685. The period of 'Restoration' was marked by a general relaxation of manners, and the Anglican Church was in firm control. The king made a formal profession of the Roman Catholic faith on his deathbed.

He was succeeded by James II who had become a Roman

Catholic about 1670. James was accepted grudgingly by the Anglican establishment, for he openly professed his Roman allegiance when he ascended to the throne in 1685. At first he tended to support the Established Church, but he soon began to favour the position of his co-religionists.

This led to his unpopularity with the population, so that the invasion of England by William, Prince of Orange (the 'Glorious Revolution') was received with general acclaim. James was deposed and exiled in 1688, and William and Mary enthroned in his stead.

When William died in 1702, he was succeeded by Queen Anne, the second daughter of James II, who continued to be brought up as an Anglican even after her father had been received into the Roman Catholic Church. At her death in 1714 the succession passed to George I.

There was a group of clergy who scrupled to take the Oath of Allegiance to William and Mary on the grounds that by so doing they would break their previous oaths to James II and his successors. They held a 'high' conception of the Church as a spiritual society with its own laws, and their mode of worship was Catholic. They were called 'Nonjurors'. The movement gradually faded in significance as most of the dissidents returned to the established Anglican Church in the course of the eighteenth century.

An important tenet of the Nonjurors was the 'divine right of kings', insisting that the monarchy was a divinely ordained institution with an hereditary right that could not be lost, for kings were accountable to God alone. Such a view was justified by various biblical texts.[1] Both reason and the fluctuating quality of successive rulers overturned this primitive doctrine in the course of the eighteenth century, which was the age of reason and known as the Enlightenment. Unlike the previous century, there was now civil tranquillity and a slow development of religious tolerance.

The early life of William Law

William Law was born in 1686 in the Northamptonshire village of King's Cliffe, twelve miles west of Peterborough, the son of a grocer and chandler who was of some standing locally. In 1705 he went to Emmanuel College, Cambridge. He was elected a Fellow in 1711 and ordained a deacon in the same year. A document that survives from Law's early Cambridge days is a set of rules for the conduct of his life, of which the first is: 'To fix deep in my mind, that I have but one business upon my hands, to seek for eternal happiness, by doing the will of God.' This is followed by seventeen more rules, all of which declare a way of dedication and self-discipline that remained characteristic of him throughout his life.

They are logical, well-written, vehement and single-minded. They are rigoristic and more reminiscent of the religious age that was passing away before a new order. They could easily have flowed from the pen of a Puritan, yet Law was a Nonjuror. The Bible and Prayer Book give sufficient scope for rigoristic attitudes.

In 1714 Queen Anne died, and George, Elector of Hanover, was invited to succeed to the English throne as George I, thus ensuring the Protestant succession and public peace. Rather than break his oath of loyalty to the House of Stuart, Law resigned his Fellowship in 1716. His chances of advancement in Church or State were ended. Daily sustenance might be problematical. This action also curtailed intercourse with his contemporaries. As a bishop he would have been involved in affairs of importance, whereas now he was restricted to the company of Nonjurors and people of no special religious background.

Law's first publication was *Three Letters to the Bishop of Bangor* in which he attacks Latitudinarism, a movement in which reason in its restricted cerebral sense was the sole arbiter of religious truth. Religious truth speaks, in addition, to the instruction of the human soul and leads to a growth of the spiritual life and good conduct in the world. Latitudinarism may certainly proceed to agnosticism, but rational belief has also been vital for understanding the past, assisting faith and enabling the Church to meet opponents on reasonable grounds. Law, as a High Churchman, could not always concede this truth, especially as he was a biblical fundamentalist.

In 1723 Law entered the home of Edward Gibbon as chaplain and private tutor to Edward's son, who was then about thirteen years old. He lived in a spacious house, with gardens and lands, at Putney in Surrey, now a part of the London borough of Wandsworth, and Law lived there until 1738–9, his employer having died in 1737. The appointment brought Law a very necessary degree of worldly security; Gibbon too was gratified by the arrangement, commending Law's sincere piety and worthiness.

The son Edward went to Emmanuel College in 1723, remaining in residence until 1725. He returned to Cambridge in 1727 and remained there until 1734; Law accompanied Edward to the University. Edward was a dull and wayward young man, but was later to be the father of the celebrated historian of the same name. Law seems to have been treated as one of the family, and was able to entertain his friends as he wished.

Law was ordained a priest by a Nonjuring bishop in 1727, but was not especially enthusiastic at having to work with a Church whose authority he doubted in relation to the Established Church, with which he had firm connections. He also was repelled by the dangers of sectarianism and factiousness, and resisted the pressing invitation to become a bishop.

During his years at Putney, in addition to writing several powerful contributions to the theological controversies of the time, he published in 1726 *A Treatise upon Christian Perfection* and in 1729 his most famous book *A Serious Call to a Devout and Holy Life*, which has been described in the *Oxford Dictionary of the Christian Church* as having had more influence than any other post-Reformation spiritual book except *The Pilgrim's Progress.*

Law's unflagging rigorism is fully expressed in this book, and his tendency to become moralistic is likely to repel the more open-minded reader. This tendency was fully in evidence in a previous pamphlet, *The Absolute Unlawfulness of Stage Entertainment*, in which the unedifying nature of theatre is emphasized, but its capacity to transfigure life with an inspiration akin to religion is overlooked. It is ironic to reflect that possibly the world's greatest dramatist, William Shakespeare, was also English. Law's Christianity was assuredly rigoristic: it lacked a civilizing humane regard; it was devoid of artistic connotation or any background of classical culture.

The main characteristic of the earlier Law was his severe harshness. It is significant that his emphasis lay on the fact that God can only love what is lovely. There is here the Dionysian influence, partly masking the gospel paradox that God does indeed love the unlovely, which is varyingly present in most mystics and Catholic writers. Part of the harshness and imbalance of *Christian Perfection* and to a lesser extent *A Serious Call* stems from the author's personality. By nature vehement, Law was in the purgative way, and he was conscious of the widespread religious formalism of the day. His motto would have been 'There must be no limit to your goodness, as your heavenly Father's goodness knows no bounds,' or more memorably expressed in the Authorised Version of the Bible, 'Be ye therefore perfect, even as your Father which is in heaven is perfect.'[2]

Half measures would never have sufficed for Law; all or nothing would have been his invariable demand. This is in fact the essence of rigorism in the domain of morality. Despite his counsel of perfection Jesus was not a rigorist. In not a few encounters with the people of everyday life he placed the self-confessed sinner far nearer the Kingdom of heaven than the self-righteous paragon. The parable of the Prodigal Son,[3] the parable of the Pharisee and the tax-collector,[4] and the incident in the Temple where the scribes and the Pharisees brought in a woman caught in the very act of adultery[5] are several instances where Jesus turned the spirit of rigorism on its head.

Jesus was not permissive in his dealings with wrong-doers, but his actions were invariably tinctured with compassion, for he could empathize with the feelings and attitudes of those around him – the scribes' and the Pharisees' self-satisfaction no less than the sinners' moral weakness. The former needed to be deflated, the latter forgiven. Law could not attain this degree of understanding, which is the reason why such a laudable book as *A Serious Call* is positively offensive to the modern reader schooled in the self-knowledge that stems from the psychological studies of Sigmund Freud and his numerous successors.

The mystical element in William Law

In these years a major change came over William Law. Though an acute and learned theologian, he had nevertheless already been described in his Cambridge days as a 'celebrated enthusiast'; he was always an emotionalist in faith and highly conscious of the dimension of mystery. He had become acquainted with Ruysbroeck, Tauler and Suso, and the *Theologia Germanica*, a spiritual treatise of the late fourteenth century written anonymously by a German priest of the Teutonic Order at Sachsenhausen, near Frankfurt-am-Main. However, the greatest of this group, Meister Eckhart, was largely unknown in England. Law was also well acquainted with others in the tradition of what he called the mystical divines, from Dionysius the Pseudo-Areopagite, who lived around 500 AD, to St John of the Cross and his own near-contemporary Archbishop Fénelon.

But it was his encounter with the works of the Silesian cobbler Jacob Boehme (1575–1624) that made the greatest impact on his life. Boehme provided him with a new symbolic language through which the narrow, severe intensity of his devotional nature was released into a new freedom of love, joy and praise. This new life was reflected not only in the development of his thought but also in a new flexibility and eloquence of his prose.

Boehme's influence is evident already in *A Demonstration of Errors* of 1737 (a work directed against the Deists), *The Grounds and Reasons of Christian Regeneration* of 1739 and two *Answers to Dr. Trapp* and *An Appeal to All That Doubt* of 1740. There followed a period of nine years while Law studied the voluminous writings of 'the illuminated Behmen'(Boehme).[6]

During this time Law moved from Putney to central London towards the end of 1738. He moved to King's Cliffe in 1740 and remained there until his death. Law was a celibate, and was the spiritual director of Hester Gibbon, the daughter of Edward Gibbon of Putney, and Mrs Hutcheson, who fulfilled her late husband's request by leading a retired life under Law's direction. They joined him in 1744 after leaving a nearby village. Law served King's Cliffe worthily, setting up a school, almshouses and a public library. His acts of charity were so renowned that paupers gathered in such a large number that the local community protested. Law stood firm, and the opposition died away, so that the following year the rector became trustee of the charities.[7]

The interesting feature of Law's spiritual life is its capacity to grow and change. He ceased to be interested in controversies within the Nonjuring community. His theological sympathies, never narrow, grew into a remarkably broad ecumenism that stretched from the Quakers to the saints of the Counter-Reformation. His earlier moral teaching, very much a matter of determination and the rational will, developed under Boehme's influence into a noble doctrine of God's love and the 'process of Christ' within each individual being. His last great work is fittingly called *The Spirit of Love*.

He still remained the same person, sometimes awkward, even rough, in his dealings, still strong in his certitudes, more a director than a listener, still eccentric in the extremity of some of his views; but with all this the Law of King's Cliffe years was clearly a man of great humility and goodwill.[8]

The moralistic writings of his middle period argue on a rational level, but Boehme was to effect a transformation: reason was to be superseded. Law becomes aware of the depths of the unconscious. He needed a system of thought which could reconcile in one structure not only the truths of biblical revelation but a rational account of the world of nature which was conformable to the science of the day and, not least, the psychological reality of the experience and process of Christian redemption as Law had come to know it. Above all it had to explain how the fact of evil in the world could be reconciled with the existence of a God of love.

Attempts have been made to find such a rational theodicy, 'to justify the ways of God to men' as Milton put it, ever since the time of Job, and no rational answer has ever been found. Law found in Boehme the elements of an explanation which for him carried overwhelming conviction and set him free to proclaim without reservation the gospel that God is all love. His righteousness and justice are themselves nothing but love, and there is no element of anger, wrath or retribution in him, and he wills only good to all his creatures. This is the core of Law's teaching.

His theodicy consists of two main elements, the one cosmological and the other psychological. The first element represents an elaboration of the very brief biblical references to the fall of the angels,[9] which led to the condensation of the spiritual realm to solid matter. Humans were then fashioned in the image of God, but soon fell, as described in Genesis 3. The fruit of this 'original sin' has been inherited by all subsequent generations. But God breathed into Adam, and so into the whole human race, the inspoken Word of Life, the seed of salvation, the spark of the divine nature which is Christ within us; and this gives each of us the ability to be redeemed, to be born again into the life of paradise. This capacity depends on the use of our free will in order to turn away from self and turn towards God. God's love is always ready to meet us and to make us one with him. However, this at-one-ment is not any kind of purchase. It is the 'process' of Christ who is already within us, the 'inward essential growth' of the divine life from the seed which is present in every person, a process which in some sense recapitulates in every individual the birth, death, resurrection and ascension of the Lord himself.

'Christ given for us is Christ given into us.' It is through our turning to God in prayer that this renewal is begun and continued within us. And correspondingly if we turn towards earthly things and direct our prayer to the creation rather than the Creator, we move inexorably towards the condition of wrath, in separation from God. Heaven and hell both begin in this life.

While the theory of evolution has made a literal acceptance of a perfect humanity that subsequently 'fell' into sin untenable, inasmuch as the ascent of humankind is believed to have its origin in the ape family, the myth of original sin is true on a strictly experiential basis. We all tend to care for ourselves, and, until circumstance teaches us that 'no man is an island, entire of itself,'[10] we will be tempted to behave dishonestly to our neighbour.

It should be understood that Law's essential concern was not to explain the origin and fate of the world and its creatures; it was to preach the gospel. The framework of theodicy was necessary not for its own sake, but for him to articulate the Christian message in terms appropriate to his own day.

In his central stress on the goodness and love of God and his view that there is in God no wrath whatever, Law comes near to his great predecessor Julian of Norwich, though there is no evidence, in the catalogue of his personal library, that he was acquainted with her writings. It is the same stress which led to his characteristic teaching about the atonement: 'that the innocent Christ did not suffer to quiet an angry Deity'; that 'Christ is in no other sense our full, perfect and sufficient atonement than as his nature and spirit are born and formed in us.' It led to his admirably ecumenical sympathies.

There are indications that the logic of his stress on love brought him at the end of his life to the 'universalist' position that in the final fire of judgement all men and all things would be saved and hell itself would be redeemed. In this respect he advanced from the position of Boehme, who accepted the wrath as well as the love of God. Boehme believed that though a soul may repent in this life, death seals our destiny. The quality of life attained here is determinative: we are bound either for heaven with God or hell with the devil.

Law believed that the wrath lay in the human only and that Christ's office was to remove that wrath in us. His sacrifice furthers the work of regeneration. Christ expiates the sins of the world by restoring human beings to their lost righteousness. Light and darkness emanate from all that is done by humanity. Darkness is the evil and misery perpetrated by fallen angels (the offspring of Lucifer) and humans. As it is from God, this darkness is without evil. It is the ground of good.

Sin leads to separation. The incomprehensible perfection of the Deity is marred by self-will, resulting in personal life as we now experience it. The self comprises covetousness, envy, pride and wrath. It is 'hell in nature'.

By the operation of the powers of eternity, light is born in the soul and reconciliation with God achieved. Thus we stand in the midst of heaven and hell with the thin wall of matter separating us from them. The new birth will be obtained by patience, meekness, humility and resignation to God; a multiplicity of rules obstruct the all-important 'simplicity of Faith'. Christ is now able to assist 'his Church, his own body' as once he assisted the outcasts and sinners. There is no way to

God but the heart. Let us 'sink down' into these four virtues, and progress in the spiritual life will be made. The Marriage Feast signifies the entrance into the highest state of union that can be between God and the soul in this life. It is the birthday of the 'Spirit of Love' in our souls, and whenever we attain it we feast on such peace and joy as blots out the remembrance of what was called by these names previously.

This attitude flows from *The Spirit of Love*, Law's crowning mystical work. Law should be included among the mystics; in *The Spirit of Prayer, The Way to Divine Knowledge* and *The Spirit of Love* he writes with such directness about God and sanctification, and makes autobiographical hints so indicative of deep penetration into God that any other description seems inadequate. Admittedly he was deeply influenced by Boehme, but he never simply copied out Boehme's revelations. He absorbed them, meditated upon them, and came to see things in terms of them. He became a visionary. It is these works rather than *A Serious Call* which stimulate the contemporary reader, other than the biblical fundamentalist.

Law's last works were the twenty-five *Letters*, and *An Address to the Clergy*. He died a few days after the last words in *An Address* were written. The year was 1761.

Law saw that 'Christ must first come as a discoverer and reprover of sin. Until we face the fact of our sin, we cannot begin to change and grow. But our very consciousness of sin is evidence that Christ is there already within us; and we can take heart from the fact that "he that discovers is the same Christ that takes away sin".'

Law also denounced our 'multiplicity of wills' as the essence of fallen nature. By this he does not mean an abandonment of any practical wishes or intentions in the world. Rather, all our separate wills should be subordinated to God's one will – just as we pray that they should in the Lord's Prayer. We can achieve this only through the spirit of prayer: 'Everything calls for it, everything is to be done in it and governed by it.' 'As humans we are constantly falling into sin, but through prayer we can be as constantly drawn back by the "divine loadstone"[11] towards our true perfection. Even though we may fully know such perfection only perhaps in rare moments of grace, we must always be facing towards the perfect life.'[12]

We have indicated William Law's place in the history of Christian mysticism and shown why his writings are relevant to folk in the twenty-first century. Law's understanding of divine love now follows in his own words.

Some find that reading one page at a time slowly and meditatively, as if one were sucking the juice out of a particularly succulent fruit, cherishing the thoughts, brings the greatest reward. This is the ancient way known as *lectio divina*.

PART TWO

William Law on Divine Love

God and Humanity

God, an eternal will

God, as considered in himself, in his holy being, before anything is brought out of him, is only an eternal will to all goodness. This is the one eternal, immutable God, that from eternity to eternity changes not. God can be neither more nor less nor anything else but an eternal will to all the goodness that is in himself and can come from him. The creation of ever so many worlds or systems of creatures adds nothing to, nor takes anything from, this immutable God. He always was and always will be the same immutable will to all goodness. As certainly as he is the creator, so certainly he is the blesser of every created thing, and can give nothing but blessing, goodness and happiness from himself, because he has in himself nothing else to give. It is much more possible for the sun to give out darkness than for God to do or be, or give out anything but blessing and goodness.

In the beginning God created the heavens and the earth.
Genesis 1.1.

God is Love

This is a glorious twofold truth, that from God considered as in himself, nothing can come from eternity to eternity, but infinite love, goodness, happiness, and glory. And also that infinite love, goodness, happiness and glory are, and will be for ever and ever flowing forth from him in the same boundless, universal, infinite manner. He is the same infinitely over-flowing fountain of love, goodness and glory after, as before the fall of any creatures. His love, and the infinite workings of it, can no more be lessened, than his power can be increased by any outward thing. No creature or number of creatures can raise any anger in him. It is as impossible as to cast terror, or darkness, or pain into him, for nothing can come into God from the creature, nothing can be in him, but that which the Holy Trinity is in itself. All creatures are products of the infinite, triune love of God. Nothing willed, and desired, and formed them, but infinite love. They all have all the happiness, beauty and excellency that an infinitely powerful love can reach out to them. The same infinite love continues still in its first creating goodness, willing, desiring, working and doing nothing with regard to all creatures, but what it willed, did and desired in the creation of them.

God is love; he who dwells in love is dwelling in God, and God in him. 1 John 4.16.

God, the boundless abyss of all that is good

God, considered in himself, is as infinitely separate from all possibility of doing hurt or willing pain to any creature as he is from a possibility of suffering pain or hurt from the hand of man.

This is because he is in himself, in his holy Trinity, nothing else but the boundless abyss of all that is good and sweet and amiable, and therefore stands in the utmost contrariety to everything that is not a blessing – in an eternal impossibility of willing and intending a moment's pain or hurt to any creature.

From this unbounded source of goodness and perfection nothing but infinite streams of blessing are perpetually flowing forth upon all creation, more plentifully incessant than rays of light streaming from the sun.

And as the sun has but one nature and can give out nothing but the blessings of light, so the holy triune God has but one nature and intent towards all creation, which is to pour forth the riches and sweetness of his divine perfections upon everything that is capable of them and according to its capacity to receive them.

And God saw all that he had made, and it was very good.
Genesis 1.31.

God, the fountain of all good

God is the Good, the unchangeable, overflowing fountain of Good that sends forth nothing but Good to all eternity. He is the love itself, the unmixed, immeasurable love, doing nothing but from love, giving nothing but gifts of love to everything that he has made; requiring nothing of all his creatures but the spirit and fruits of that love which brought them into being.

Oh, how sweet is this contemplation of the height and depth of the riches of divine love! With what attraction must it draw every thoughtful man to return love for love to this overflowing fountain of boundless goodness!

View every part of our redemption, from Adam's first sin to the resurrection of the dead, and you will find nothing but successive mysteries of that first love which created angels and men. All the mysteries of the gospel are only so many marks and proofs of God's desiring to make his love triumph in the removal of sin and disorder from all nature and creatures.

I shall give praise to you, Lord, with my whole heart, I shall recount all your marvellous deeds. Psalm 9.1.

Divine love

Divine love is perfect peace and joy, it is a freedom from all disquiet, it is all content and mere happiness and makes everything to rejoice in itself. Love is the Christ of God. Wherever it comes, it comes as the blessing and happiness of every natural life, as the restorer of every lost perfection, a redeemer from all evil, a fulfiller of all righteousness, and a peace of God which passes all understanding.

Through all the universe of things nothing is uneasy, unsatisfied or restless but because it is not governed by love, or because its nature has not reached or attained the full birth of the spirit of love. For when that is done every hunger is satisfied, and all complaining, murmuring, accusing, resenting, revenging and striving are as totally suppressed and overcome as the coldness, thickness and horror of darkness are suppressed and overcome by the breaking-forth of the light.

If you ask why the spirit of love cannot be displeased, cannot be disappointed, cannot complain, accuse, resent or murmur, it is because divine love desires nothing but itself, it is its own good, it has all when it has itself, because nothing is good but itself and its own working; for love is God and he that dwells in God dwells in love.

I give you a new commandment: love one another;
as I have loved you, so you are to love one another. John 13.34.

The healing power of love

Love, like the spirit of God rides upon the wings of the wind, and is in union and communion with all the saints that are in heaven and on earth.

Love is quite pure; it has no by-ends; it seeks not its own. It has only one will, and that is to give itself into everything and overcome all evil with good.

Lastly, love is the Christ of God; it comes down from heaven; it regenerates the soul from above; it blots out all transgressions; it takes from death its sting, from the devil his power, and from the serpent his poison. It heals all the infirmities of our earthly birth. It gives eyes to the blind, ears to the deaf, and makes the dumb to speak. It cleanses the lepers and casts out devils, and puts man in paradise before he dies.

For this son of mine was dead and has come back to life;
he was lost and is found. Luke 15.24.

Irresistible love

Nothing is so strong, so irresistible as divine love. It brought about all creation; it kindles all the life of heaven, it is the song of all the angels of God. It has redeemed all the world; it seeks for every sinner upon earth; it embraces all the enemies of God; and, from the beginning to the end of time, the one work of providence is the one work of love.

Ask what God is? his name is Love; he is the good, the perfection, the peace, the joy, the glory, and the blessing of every life. Ask what Christ is? He is the universal remedy of all evil broken forth in nature and creature. He is the destruction of misery, sin, darkness, death and hell. He is the resurrection and life of all fallen nature. He is the unwearied compassion, the long-suffering pity, the never-ceasing mercifulness of God to every want and infirmity of human nature. He is the breathing-forth of the heart, life and spirit of God, into all the dead race of Adam. He is the seeker, the finder, the restorer of all that was lost and dead to the life of God. He is the Love that from Cain to the end of time prays for all murderers, the Love that willingly suffers and dies among thieves that thieves may have a life with him in paradise; the Love that visits publicans, harlots and sinners, and wants and seeks to forgive where most is to be forgiven.

A Samaritan who was going that way came upon him, and when he saw him he was moved to pity. Luke 10.33.

The spirit of love

All religion is the spirit of love; all its gifts and graces are the gifts and graces of love; it has no breath, no life, but the life of love.

Nothing exalts, nothing purifies but the fire of love. Nothing changes death into life, earth into heaven, men into angels, but love alone. Love breathes the spirit of God; its words and works are the inspiration of God. Love speaks not of itself, but the Word, the eternal Word of God speaks in it. All that love speaks, that God speaks, because love is God.

Love is heaven revealed in the soul; it is light and truth; it is infallible; it has no errors, for all errors are the want of love. Love has no more of pride than light has of darkness; it stands and bears all its fruits from a depth and root of humility.

Love is of no sect or party; it neither makes nor admits of any bounds; you may as easily enclose the light or shut up the air of the world in one place, as confine love to a sect or party. It lives in the liberty, the universality, the impartiality of heaven.

There is nothing love cannot face; there is no limit to its faith, its hope, its endurance. 1 Corinthians 13.7.

God's universal love

Some people have an idea of the Christian religion as if God was so full of anger against fallen man that nothing but the blood of his only begotten Son could satisfy his vengeance. These are miserable mistakers of the divine nature and miserable reproachers of his great love and goodness.

For God is love, yea all love; and so all love that nothing but love can come from him. The Christian religion is nothing else but an open, full manifestation of his universal love towards all mankind.

As the light of the sun has only one common nature towards all objects that can receive it, so God has only one common nature of goodness towards all created nature, breaking forth in infinite flames of love upon every part of creation and calling everything to the highest happiness it is capable of.

God so loved man, when his fall was foreseen, that he chose him to salvation in Christ Jesus before the foundation of the world. When man was actually fallen, God was so without all anger towards him that he sent his only begotten Son into the world to redeem him. Therefore God has no nature towards man but love, and all that he does to man is love.

God so loved the world that he gave his only Son,
that everyone who has faith in him may not perish but have eternal life.
John 3.16.

Governed by love

Through all the universe of things, nothing is uneasy, unsatisfied, or restless, but because it is not governed by love, or because its nature has not reached or attained the full birth of the Spirit of Love ...

Just so much, and so far, as you are freed from the folly of all earthly affections, from all disquiet, trouble, and complaint about this or that, just so much and so far is the Spirit of Love come to life in you. For Divine Love is a new life and new nature, and introduces you into a new world. It puts an end to all your former opinions, notions and tempers, it opens new senses in you, and makes you see high to be low, and low to be high, wisdom to be foolishness, and foolishness wisdom. It makes prosperity and adversity, praise and dispraise, to be equally nothing. 'When I was a child,' says the apostle, 'I thought as a child, I spoke as a child, but when I became a man, I put away childish things.' Whilst man is under the power of nature, governed only by worldly wisdom, his life, however old he may be, is quite childish; everything about him only awakens childish thoughts and pursuits in him. All that he sees and hears, all that he desires or fears, likes or dislikes, that which he gets, and that which he loses, that which he has, and that which he has not, serve only to carry him from this fiction of evil to that fiction of good, from one vanity of peace to another vanity of trouble. But when Divine Love is born in the soul, all childish images of good and evil are done away, and all the sensibility of them is lost, as the stars lose their visibility when the sun is risen.

All I know is this: I was blind and now I can see. John 9.25.

The height and depth of eternity in you

O man! consider yourself. Here you stand in the earnest, perpetual strife of good and evil. All nature is continually at work to bring about the great redemption. The whole creation is travailing in pain and laborious working to be delivered from the vanity of time. And will you be asleep?

Everything you hear or see says nothing, shows nothing to you but what either eternal light or eternal darkness has brought forth. For as day and night divide the whole of our time, so heaven and hell divide the whole of our thoughts, words and actions. Stir which way you will, do or design what you will, you must be an agent with the one or the other.

You cannot stand still because you live in the perpetual workings of temporal and eternal nature. If you work not with the good, the evil that is in nature carries you along with it. You have the height and depth of eternity in you, and therefore, be doing what you will, in either the closet, the field, the shop or the church, you are sowing that which grows and must be reaped in eternity.

The heavens tell out the glory of God, heaven's vault makes known his handiwork. Psalm 19.1.

The breath and life of the triune God

There is in the soul of every man the fire and light and love of God, though lodged in a state of hiddenness, inactivity and death until something or other, human or divine, Moses and the prophets, Christ or his apostles, uncover its life within us.

For the soul of every man is the breath and life of the triune God, and as such a partaker of the divine nature. All this divinity is unfelt because it is overpowered by the workings of flesh and blood until such time as distress, or grace, or both give flesh and blood a shock, open the long-shut-up eyes, and force a man to find something in himself that sense and reason, while at quiet, were not aware of.

To them he chose to make known what a wealth of glory is offered to the Gentiles in this secret purpose: Christ in you: the hope of glory. Colossians 1.27.

God in man

Poor and miserable as this life is, we have all of us free access to all that is great, and good, and happy. We carry within ourselves a key to all the treasures that heaven has to bestow upon us. We starve in the midst of plenty, groan under infirmities with the remedy in our own hand, live and die without knowing and feeling anything of the one only Good, whilst we have it in our power to know and enjoy it in as great a reality as we know and feel the power of this world over us.

For heaven is as near to our souls as this world is to our bodies; and we are created, we are redeemed, to have our conversation in it. God, the only Good of all intelligent natures, is not an absent or distant God, but is more present in and to our souls than our own bodies. We are strangers to heaven and without God in the world, for this reason only, that we are void of that spirit of prayer which alone can unite, and never fails to unite us with the one only Good, and to open heaven and the kingdom of God within us.

A root set in the finest soil, in the best climate, and blessed with all that sun, and air, and rain can do for it, is not in so sure a way of its growth to perfection as every man may be whose spirit aspires after all that which God is ready and infinitely desirous to give him. For the sun meets not the springing bud that stretches towards him with half that certainty as God, the source of all good, communicates himself to the soul that longs to partake of him.

For all who are led by the Spirit of God are sons of God.
Romans 8.14.

Two states or forms of life

There are, in all the possibility of things, but two states or forms of life. The one is nature and the other is God manifested in nature; and as God and nature are both within you, so you have it in your power to love and work with which you will, but are under a necessity of doing either the one or the other. There is no standing still. Life goes on and is always bringing forth its realities, which ever way it goes.

The properties of nature are, and can be, nothing else in themselves but a restless hunger, disquiet and blind strife for they know not what, until the properties of light and love have got possession of them. Blind nature does all the work, and must be the doer of it, until the Christ of God is born in the natural man.

Goodness is only a sound, and virtue a mere strife of natural passions, until the spirit of love is the breath of everything that lives and moves in the heart. For love is the one only blessing, goodness and God of nature; and you have no true religion, are no worshipper of the one true God, but in and by that spirit of love which is God himself living and working in you.

No man can serve two masters; for either he will hate the first and love the second, or he will be devoted to the first and despise the second. You cannot serve God and Money. Matthew 6.24.

All is within man

Now, that which we are here taught is the whole end of all Scripture. All that is there said, however learnedly read or studied by Hebrew or Greek skill, fails of its only end till it leads and brings us to an Essential God within us, to feel and find all that which the Scriptures speak of God, of man, of life and death, of good and evil, of heaven and hell, as essentially verified in our own souls.

For all is within man that can be either good or evil to him. God within him is his divine life, his divine light, and his divine love. Satan within him is his life of self, of earthly wisdom, of diabolical falseness, anger, pride, and vanity of every kind. There is no middle way between these two. He that is not under the power of the one is under the power of the other.

The smelting pot for silver, the crucible for gold, but the Lord it is who assays the heart. Proverbs 17.3.

The purgatory of the whole creation

This is a certain truth that hell and death, curse and misery, can never cease or be removed from the creation until the will of the creature is again as it came from God, and is only a spirit of love that wills nothing but goodness.

All the whole fallen creation, stand it never so long, must groan and travail in pain, this must be its purgatory until everything contrary to the divine will is entirely taken from every creature.

Which is only saying that all the powers and properties of nature are a misery to themselves, can only work in disquiet and anger, until the birth of the Son of God brings them under the dominion and power of the spirit of love.

The universe itself is to be freed from the shackles of mortality and is to enter upon the glorious liberty of the children of God.
Romans 8.21.

The origin of Evil

God manifested in nature is the only blessing, happiness and perfection of nature. Therefore the creature that in the working of its will is turned from God must have as great a change brought forth in it as that of heaven changed into hell. Hence we see the deep ground and absolute necessity of the Christian redemption by a birth from above of the light and spirit of God, demonstrated in the most absolute degree of certainty.

It is because all nature is in itself nothing but a hungry, angry fire of life, a tormenting darkness, unless the light and spirit of God kindle it into a kingdom of heaven. And therefore the fallen soul can have no possible relief or redemption, it must be to all eternity a hungry, dark, fiery, tormenting spirit of life, unless the light, or Son, and Spirit of God be born again in it. Hence it also follows that in all the possibility of things there is and can be but one happiness and one misery. The one misery is nature and creature left to itself. The one happiness is the life, the light, the Spirit of God, manifested in nature and creature. This is the true meaning of those words of our Lord, there is but One that is good, and that is God.

Here we see the plain and true original of all evil, without any perplexity or imputation upon God:

– That evil is nothing else but the anger and fire and darkness of nature broken off from God;

– That the punishment, the pain or the hell of sin is no designedly prepared or arbitrary penalty inflicted by God, but the natural and necessary state of the creature that leaves or turns from God.

Let us build ourselves a city and a tower with its top in the heavens and make a name for ourselves . . . The Lord came down to see the city and the tower, and said, 'Here they are, one people with a single language, and now they have started to do this; from now on nothing they have a mind to do will be beyond their reach.' Genesis 11.4–6.

The Fall

Though comforts of this world keep even the worst of men from any constant, strong awareness of that angry, fiery, dark and self-tormenting nature that is the very essence of every fallen unregenerate soul, yet every man in the world has, more or less, frequent and strong intimations given him, that so it is with him in the inmost ground of his soul. How many inventions are some people forced to have recourse to in order to keep off a certain inner uneasiness which they are afraid of, and know not whence it comes? Alas, 'tis because there is a dark aching fire within them, which has never had its proper relief, and is trying to reveal itself, and calling out for help at every cessation of worldly joy.

Why are some people, when under heavy disappointments or some great worldly shame, unable to bear themselves, and desirous of death of any kind? It's because the soul is left to its own dark, fiery, raging nature, and would destroy the body at any rate, rather than continue under such a sensibility of its own angry, self-tormenting fire. Who has not at one time or other felt a sourness, an anger, a selfishness, an envy, and a pride, which he could not tell what to do with or how to bear, rising up in him without his consent, casting a blackness over all his thoughts, and then as suddenly going off again, either by the cheerfulness of the sun or air, or some agreeable accident, and again at times as suddenly returning upon him? Sufficient indications are these to every man that there is a dark guest within him, often lulled asleep by worldly light and amusements, yet such as will, in spite of everything, show itself. The which, if it has not its proper relief in this life, must be his torment in eternity. It was for the sake of this hidden hell within us that our blessed Lord said when on earth, and says now to every soul, 'Come unto me, all ye that labour and are heavy laden, and I will give you rest.'

God has forbidden us to eat the fruit of that tree or even to touch it;
if we do, we shall die. Genesis 3.3.

The birth of Jesus

No sooner is the finite desire of the creature in motion towards God, but the infinite desire of God is united with, co-operates with it.

When therefore the first spark of a desire after God arises in your soul, cherish it with all your care, give all your heart into it. It is nothing less than a touch of the divine loadstone that is to draw you out of the vanity of time into the riches of eternity.

Get up therefore and follow it as gladly as the wise men of the East followed the star from heaven that appeared to them. It will do for you as the star did for them. It will lead you to the birth of Jesus, not in a stable at Bethlehem in Judaea, but to the birth of Jesus in the dark centre of your own fallen soul.

The star went ahead of them until it stopped above the place where the child lay. They were overjoyed at the sight of it and, entering the house, they saw the child with Mary his mother and bowed low in homage to him; they opened their treasure chests and presented gifts to him: gold, frankincense and myrrh. Matthew 2.10-11.

The heart of man

If you have never yet owned him, if you have wandered from him as far as the Prodigal Son from his father's house, yet he is still with you. He is the gift of God to you, and if you will turn to him and ask of him, he has living water for you.

Poor sinner! consider the treasure you have within you. The Saviour of the world, the eternal Word of God, lies hid in you as a spark of the divine nature which is to overcome sin and death and hell within you and generate the life of heaven again in your soul. Turn to your heart, and your heart will find its saviour, its God within itself.

You see, hear, and feel nothing of God, because you seek for him in books, in controversies, in the church, and in outward exercises. But you will not find him there till you have first found him in your heart. Seek for him in your heart and you will never seek in vain; for there he dwells. There is the seat of his light and holy spirit. For this turning to the light and spirit of God within you is your only true turning to God.

There is no other way of finding him. Though God be everywhere present, yet he is only present to you in the deepest and most central part of your soul. Your natural senses cannot possess God, or unite you to him. Your inner faculties of understanding, will and memory, can only reach after God, but cannot be the place of his habitation in you. But there is a root or depth in you whence all these faculties come forth as lines from a centre, or as branches from the body of the tree.

This depth is called the centre, the fund, or bottom of the soul. This depth is the unity, the eternity – I had almost said the infinity – of your soul; for it is so infinite that nothing can satisfy it or give it any rest but the infinity of God.

Then they said to one another, 'Were not our hearts on fire as he talked with us on the road and explained the scriptures to us?'
Luke 24.32.

A seed of salvation

In this depth of the soul the Holy Trinity brought forth its own living image in the first created man, bearing in himself a living representation of Father, Son, and Holy Ghost, and this was his dwelling in God and God in him.

This was the kingdom of God within him and made Paradise in the outside world. But the day that Adam ate of the forbidden earthly tree, in that day he absolutely died to this kingdom of God within him. This depth or centre of his soul, having lost its God, was shut up in death and darkness and became a prisoner in an earthly animal that only excelled its brethren, the beasts, in an upright form and serpentine subtlety. Thus ended the fall of man.

But from that moment that the God of mercy inspoke into Adam the Bruiser of the Serpent, from that moment all the riches and treasures of the divine nature came again into man, as a seed of salvation sown into the centre of the soul, and only lies hidden there in every man till he desires to rise from his fallen state and to be born again from above.

Awake, then, you that sleep, and Christ, who from all eternity has been espoused to your soul, shall give you light. Begin to search and dig in your own field for this pearl of eternity that lies hidden in it; it cannot cost you too much, nor can you buy it too dear, for it is *all*. When you have found it, you will know that all which you have sold or given away for it is as mere a nothing as a bubble upon the water.

Repent, for the kingdom of Heaven is upon you! Matthew 3.2.

Hubris and Prayer

The will of God and the harmony of creation

God created everything to partake of his own nature, to have some degree and share of his own life and happiness. Nothing can be good or evil, happy or unhappy, but as it does or does not stand in the same degree of divine life in which it was created, receiving in God and from God all that good that it is capable of, and co-operating with him according to the nature of its powers and perfections.

As soon as it turns to itself and would, as it were, have a sound of its own, it breaks off from the divine harmony and falls into the misery of its own discord. All its workings then are only so many sorts of torment or ways of feeling its own poverty.

The redemption of mankind can then only be effected, the harmony of the creation can then only be restored, when the will of God is the will of every creature.

For this reason our blessed Lord, having taken upon him a created nature, so continually declares against the doing of anything of himself and always appeals to the will of God as the only motive and end of everything he did, saying that it was his meat and drink to do the will of him that sent him.

I do not speak on my own authority, but the Father who sent me has himself commanded me what to say and how to speak. I know that his commands are eternal life. What the Father has said to me, therefore − that is what I speak. John 12.49−50.

Eternal, divine powers

Thinking and willing are eternal, they never began to be. Nothing can think, or will now, in which there was not will and thought from all eternity.

And herein lies the true ground and depth of the uncontrollable freedom of our will and thoughts: they must have a self-motion, and self-direction, because they came out of the self-existent God. They are eternal, divine powers, that never began to be, and therefore cannot begin to be in subjection to any thing. That which thinks and wills in the soul, is that very same unbeginning breath which thought and willed in God, before it was breathed into the form of an human soul; and so it is, that will and thought cannot be bounded or constrained.

God created human beings in his own image; in the image of God he created them; male and female he created them. Genesis 1.27.

The free will of man

The will is not a made thing, or a thing that came out of some different state into the state of a will. But the free will of man is a true and real birth from the free, eternal, uncreated Will of God, which willed to have a creaturely offspring of itself, or to see itself in a creaturely state. And therefore the will of man has the nature of Divine freedom. It has the nature of eternity, and the nature of omnipotence in it, because it is what it is, and has what it has, as a spark, a ray, a genuine birth of the eternal, free, omnipotent Will of God.

As the Will of God is superior to and rules over all nature, so the will of man, derived from the Will of God, is superior to and rules over all his own nature. Thence, as to itself, and so far as its own nature reaches, it has the freedom and omnipotence of that Will from which it is descended, and can have or receive nothing but what itself does or works, in and to itself. And every will, wherever found, is the birth and effect of some antecedent will, for will can only proceed from will, till you come to the first working Will, which is God Himself.

Our Father in heaven, may your name be hallowed; your kingdom come, your will be done, on earth as in heaven. Matthew 6.9–10.

The state of our will

It is the state of our will that makes the state of our life; when we receive anything from God and do everything for God, everything does us the same good and helps us to the same degree of happiness.

Sickness and health, prosperity and adversity, bless and pacify such a soul in the same degree. As it turns everything towards God, so everything becomes divine to it. For he that seeks God in everything is sure to find God in everything.

When we thus live wholly unto God, God is wholly ours and we are happy in all that happiness of God. For in uniting with him in heart and will and spirit, we are united to all that he is and has in himself.

This is the purity and perfection of life that we pray for in the Lord's Prayer, that God's Kingdom may come and his will be done in us as it is in heaven. And this, we may be sure, is not only necessary but also attainable by us, or our Saviour would not have made it a part of our daily prayer.

The course of the righteous is like morning light, growing ever brighter till it is broad day. Proverbs 4.18.

The only opener

The will of the creature is the only opener of all evil or good in the creature. The will stands between God and nature, and must in all its workings unite either with God or with nature.

When the desire, the delight and longing of the soul, is set upon earthly things, then humanity is degraded, is fallen from God, and the life of the soul is made as bestial as the life of the body. For the creature can be neither higher nor lower, neither better nor worse, than as the will works. For you are to observe that the will has a divine power; what it desires, that it takes, and of that it eats and lives.

Wherever and in whatever the working will chooses to dwell and delight, that becomes the soul's food, its condition, its body, its clothing and habitation. For all these are the true and certain effects and powers of the working will. Nothing goes, or can go, with a man into heaven, nothing follows him into hell, but that in which it was fed, nourished and clothed in this life.

Father, if it be your will, take this cup from me. Yet not my will but yours be done. Luke 22.42.

God's will is the only good

The soul is only so far cleansed from its corruption, so far delivered from the power of sin, and so far purified, as it has renounced all its own will and own desire to have nothing, receive nothing and be nothing but what the one will of God chooses for it and does to it.

This and this alone is the true Kingdom of God opened in the soul when stripped of all selfishness. It has only one love and one will in it, when it has no motion or desire but what branches from the love of God and resigns itself wholly to the will of God.

There is nothing evil or the cause of evil to either man or devil but his own will; there is nothing good in itself but the will of God.

He, therefore, who renounces his own will turns away from all evil; and he who gives himself up wholly to the will of God puts himself in the possession of all that is good.

God who searches our inmost being knows what the Spirit means,
because he pleads for God's people as God himself wills.
Romans 8.27.

The multiplicity of wills

'Your Kingdom come, your will be done' is the one will and one hunger that feeds the soul with the life-giving bread of heaven. This will is always fulfilled. It cannot possibly be sent empty away, for God's Kingdom must manifest itself with all its riches in that soul which wills nothing else.

If you have no inner peace, if religious comfort is still wanting, it is because you have more wills than one. For the multiplicity of wills is the very essence of fallen nature, and all its evil, misery and separation from God lies in it; and as soon as you return to and allow only this one will, you are returned to God, and must find the blessedness of his Kingdom within you.

Nothing can put an end to this multiplicity of wills in fallen man which is his death to God, nothing can be the resurrection of the divine nature within him, which is his only salvation, but the cross of Christ - not that wooden cross on which he was crucified, but that cross on which he was crucified through the whole course of his life in the flesh. It is our fellowship with him on this cross through the whole course of our lives that is our union with him.

A thief comes only to steal, kill and destroy; I have come that they may have life, and may have it in all its fullness. John 10.10.

All equally selfish

A religious faith that is uninspired, a hope, or love that proceeds not from the immediate working of the divine nature within us, can no more do any divine good to our souls, or unite them with the goodness of God, than an hunger after earthly food can feed us with the immortal bread of heaven. All that the natural or uninspired man does, or can do, in the church has no more of the truth or power of divine worship in it, than that which he does in the field or shop, through a desire of riches.

The reason is, because all the acts of the natural man, whether relating to matters of religion or the world, must be equally selfish, and there is no possibility of their being otherwise. For self-love, self-esteem, self-seeking, and living wholly to self, are as strictly the whole of all that is or possibly can be in the natural man. As in the natural beast, the one can no more be better, or act above this nature, than the other.

Neither can any creature be in a better, or higher state than this, till something supernatural is found in it. This supernatural something, called in scripture the Word, or Spirit, or Inspiration of God, is that alone from which man can have the first good thought about God, or the least power of having more heavenly desires in his spirit, than he has in his flesh.

There an angel of the Lord appeared to him as a fire blazing out from a bush. Exodus 3.2.

Self

Self is the only root, or rather the sum-total of all sin. Every sin that can be named is centred in it, and the creature can sin no higher than he can live to self ... Man's intellectual faculties are, by the fall, in a much worse state than his natural animal appetites, and require a much greater self-denial. To know all this to be strictly the truth, no more need be known than these two things:

(1) That our salvation consists wholly in being saved from ourselves, or from that which we are by nature;

(2) That in the whole nature of things nothing could be this salvation or Saviour to us, except such an humility of God manifested in human nature as is beyond all expression. Hence, the first unalterable term of this Saviour to fallen man is this: 'except a man denies himself, forsakes all that he has, yes, all his own life, he cannot be my disciple.' And to show that this is but the beginning or ground of man's salvation, the Saviour adds: 'Learn of me, for I am meek and lowly of heart.'

Self is the whole evil of fallen nature; self-denial is our capacity of being saved; humility is our saviour. Then old Adam with all his ignorance is cast out of him. When Christ's humility is learnt, then he has the very mind of Christ, and that which brings him forth a Son of God ... Self is the root, the tree, and the branches of all the evils of our fallen state. We are without God, because we are in the life of self. Self-love, self-esteem, and self-seeking are the very essence and life of pride. All the vices of fallen angels and men have their birth and power in the pride of self ... On the other hand, all the virtues of the heavenly life are the virtues of humility. Not a joy, or glory, or praise in heaven, but what it is through humility. It is humility alone that makes the unpassable gulf between heaven and hell.

When he heard this his heart sank, for he was a very rich man . . . Jesus said, 'How hard it is for the wealthy to enter the kingdom of God! It is easier for a camel to go through the eye of a needle than for a rich man to enter the kingdom of God.' Luke 18.23–5.

One way, one truth and one life

The truth is this: pride must die in you or nothing of heaven can live in you. Under the banner of this truth give up your selves to the meek and humble Spirit of the holy Jesus, the overcomer of all fire and pride and anger. This is the one way, the one truth, and the one life. There is no other open door into the sheepfold of God. Humility must sow the seed, or there can be no reaping in heaven.

So much as you have of pride, so much you have of the fallen angel alive in you. So much as you have of true humility, so much you have of the Lamb of God within you. Could you see what a sweet, divine, transforming power there is in humility, what a heavenly water of life it gives to the fiery breath of your soul, how it expels the poison of your fallen nature, and makes room for the spirit of God to live in you, you would rather wish to be the footstool of all the world than to want the smallest degree of pride.

Look not at pride only as an unbecoming temper; nor at humility only as a decent virtue; for the one is death and the other is life; the one is all hell and the other is all heaven.

'Learn of me for I am meek and lowly of heart.' If this lesson is unlearnt, we must be said to have left our Master, as those disciples did who went back and walked no more with him.

The centurion replied, 'Sir, I am not worthy to have you under my roof. You need only say the word and my servant will be cured.'
Matthew 8.8.

Pride

If selfish pride is the spirit of a life, he understands nothing, he feels nothing, but as his pride is capable of being affected by it. His working will, which is the life of his soul, lives and works only in the element of pride. He can talk of a scripture God, a scripture Christ and heaven, but these are only the ornamental furniture of his brain, whilst pride is the God of his heart.

We are told that God resists the proud and gives grace to the humble. This is not to be understood as if God, by an arbitrary will, only chose to deal thus with the proud and humble man. Oh, no; the true ground is this: the resistance is on the part of man. Pride resists God, it rejects him, it turns from him, and chooses to worship and adore something else instead of him. Humility leaves all for God, falls down before him and opens all the doors of the heart for his entrance into it. This is the only sense in which God resists the proud, and gives grace to the humble.

A prophet never lacks honour, except in his home town and in his own family. Matthew 13.57.

The inner strong man of pride

The inner strong man of pride, the diabolical self, has his higher works within; he dwells in the strength of the heart, and has every power and faculty of the soul offering continual incense to him.

His memory, his will, his understanding, his imagination are always at work for him and for no one else. His memory is the faithful repository of all the fine things that self has ever done; and lest anything of them should be lost or forgotten, she is continually setting them before his eyes. His will, though it has all the world before it, yet goes after nothing but as self sends it. His understanding is ever looking out for new projects to enlarge the dominions of self; and if this falls, imagination comes in as the last and truest support of self; she makes him a king and mighty lord of castles in the air.

This is that full-born natural self that must be pulled out of the heart and totally denied, or there can be no disciple of Christ; which is only saying this plain truth, that the apostate, self-idolatrous nature of the old man must be put off, or there can be no new creature in Christ.

The Pharisee stood up and prayed this prayer: 'I thank you, God, that I am not like the rest of mankind – greedy, dishonest, adulterous – or, for that matter, like this tax-collector. I fast twice a week; I pay tithes on all that I get.' Luke 18.11–12.

Worldliness

Every sin, be it what kind it will, is only a branch of the worldly spirit that lives in us. There is only one that is good, says our Lord, and that is God. There is only one life that is good, and that life is the life of God in heaven. Choose any life but the life of God in heaven, and you choose death; for death is nothing else but the loss of the life of God.

The spirit of the soul is in itself nothing else but a spirit breathed forth from the life of God, and for this end only; that the life of God, the nature of God, the working of God, the tempers of God, might be manifested in it. God could not create man to have a will of his own, and a life of his own, different from the life and will that is in himself. This is more impossible than for a good tree to bring forth corrupt fruit. The life of God must be the life of the soul, if the soul is to unite with God.

A worldly spirit is not to be considered as a single sin, or as something that may consist with some real degrees of Christian goodness, but as a state of real death to the kingdom and life of God in our souls. Management, prudence, or an artful trimming between God and mammon, are here all in vain. It is not only the grossness of an outward visible, worldly behaviour, but the spirit, the prudence, the subtlety, the wisdom of this world, that is our separation from the life of God. Though heaven and hell are both within us, yet we feel neither the one nor the other so long as the spirit of this world reigns in us. The natural man, says the apostle, receives not the things of the spirit of God, they are foolishness to him. He cannot know them, because they are spiritually discerned; that is, they can only be discerned by that spirit which he has not.

When Herod saw Jesus he was greatly pleased; he had heard about him and had long been wanting to see him in the hope of witnessing some miracle performed by him. Luke 23.8.

Covetousness, envy, pride and anger

Covetousness, envy, pride and anger are the four elements of self, or nature, or hell, all of them inseparable from it.

Now covetousness, pride and envy are not three different things, but only three different names for the restless workings of one and the same will or desire which, as it differently torments itself, takes these different names.

And therefore, when fallen from God, this desire's three first births, which are quite inseparable from it, are covetousness, envy and pride.

It must covet because it is a desire proceeding from want. It must envy because it is a desire turned to self. It must assume and arrogate because it is a desire founded on a real lack of exaltation or a higher state.

Now anger, which is a fourth birth from these three, can have no existence until some or all of these three are contradicted, or have something done to them that is contrary to their will; and then it is that anger is necessarily born, and not until then.

Make no mistake about this: God is not to be fooled; everyone reaps what he sows. If he sows in the field of his unspiritual nature, he will reap from it a harvest of corruption; but if he sows in the field of the Spirit, he will reap from it a harvest of eternal life.
Galatians 6.7–8.

The life of pride

Self is the root, the tree, and the branches of all the evils of our fallen state. We are without God, because we are in the life of self. Self-love, self-esteem, and self-seeking are the very essence and life of pride ...

What is, then, or in what lies the great struggle for eternal life? It all lies in the strife between pride and humility: all other things, be they what they will, are but as under-workmen. Pride and humility are the two master-powers, the two kingdoms in strife for the eternal possession of man ...

If you would see the deepest root and iron strength of pride and self-adoration, you must enter into the dark chamber of man's fiery soul. There the light of God – which alone gives humility and meek submission to all created spirits – being extinguished by the death which Adam died, Satan, or self-exaltation (which is the same thing), became the strong man that kept possession of the house till a stronger than he should come upon him ...

This is that full-born natural self that must be pulled out of the heart and totally denied, or there can be no disciple of Christ. Which is only saying this plain truth, that the apostate, self-idolatrous nature of the old man must be put off, or there can be no new creature in Christ.

Pride goes before disaster, and arrogance before a fall. Proverbs 16.18.

Resentment

To rejoice in a resentment gratified appears now to me to be quite frightful. For what is it in reality but rejoicing that my own serpent of self has new life and strength given to it, and that the precious Lamb of God is denied entrance to my soul?

For this is the strict truth of the matter. To give in to resentment and willingly to gratify it is calling up the courage of your own serpent and truly helping it to be more stout, valiant and successful in you.

On the other hand, to give up resentment of every kind and on every occasion, however artfully, beautifully, outwardly coloured, and to sink down into the humility of meekness under all contrariety, contradiction and injustice, always turning the other cheek to the smiter, however haughty, is the best of all prayers, the surest of all means to have nothing but Christ living and working in you, as the Lamb of God that takes away every sin that ever had power over your soul.

Jesus said, 'Father, forgive them; they do not know what they are doing.' Luke 23.34.

Faith

We believe in a Saviour, not because we feel an absolute want
of one, but because we have been told there is one, and that it
would be a rebellion against God to reject him. We believe in
Christ as our Atonement, just as we believe he cast seven devils
out of Mary Magdalene, and so are no more helped, delivered
and justified by believing that he is our Atonement than by
believing that he cured Mary Magdalene.

True faith is coming to Jesus Christ to be saved and delivered
from a sinful nature, as the Canaanitish woman came to him
and would not be denied.

All things will be dull and heavy, difficult and impossible to
us, we shall toil all the night and take nothing, we shall be tired
with resisting temptations, grow old and stiff in our sins and
infirmities, if we do not with a strong, full, loving and joyful
assurance, seek and come to Christ for every kind and degree of
strength, salvation and redemption. We must come to Christ, as
the blind, the sick and the leprous came to him, expecting all
from him, and nothing from themselves. When we have this
faith, then it is that Christ can do all his mighty works in us.

Faith gives substance to our hopes and convinces us of realities we do not
see. Hebrews 11.1.

The great work already begun

It is clear that no one can fail of the benefit of Christ's salvation but through an unwillingness to have it, and from the same spirit and tempers which made the Jews unwilling to receive it. If you would still further know how this great work, the birth of Christ, is to be effected in you, then let this joyful truth be told you, that this great work is already begun in every one of us.

For this holy Jesus that is to be formed in you, that is to be the Saviour and new life of your soul, that is to raise you out of the darkness of death into the light of life and give you power to become a son of God, is already within you, living, stirring, calling, knocking at the door of your heart, and wanting nothing but your own faith and good will, to have as real a birth and form in you as he had in the Virgin Mary.

For the eternal Word or Son of God did not first begin to be the Saviour of the world when he was born in Bethlehem of Judea. Rather that Word which became man in the Virgin Mary did from the beginning of the world enter as a word of life, a seed of salvation, into the first father of mankind, was inspoken into him as an ingrafted word under the name and character of a Bruiser of the Serpent's head. Hence it is that Christ said to his disciples, 'The Kingdom of God is within you'. That is, the divine nature is within you, given to your first father, into the light of his life, and from him rising up in the life of every son of Adam.

Jesus said, 'In very truth I tell you, before Abraham was born, I am.'
John 8.58.

Immanuel

The holy Jesus is said to be the 'Light which lights every man that comes into the world'. Not as he was born at Bethlehem, not as he had a human form upon earth; in these respects he could not be said to have been the light of every man that comes into the world. Rather, as he was that eternal Word by which all things were created, which was the life and light of all things, and which had as a second Creator entered again into fallen man as a Bruiser of the Serpent; in this respect, it was truly said of our Lord, when on earth, that he was that Light which lights every man that comes into the world.

For he was really and truly all this, as he was the Immanuel, the God with us, given unto Adam and in him to all his offspring. See here the beginning and glorious extent of the Catholic Church of Christ. It takes in all the world. It is God's unlimited, universal mercy to all mankind.

Every human creature, as sure as he is born of Adam, has a birth of the Bruiser of the Serpent within him, and so is infallibly in covenant with God through Jesus Christ. Hence also it is that the holy Jesus is appointed to be Judge of all the world. It is because all mankind, all nations and languages have, in him and through him, been put into covenant with God and made capable of resisting the evil of their fallen nature.

In the beginning the Word already was. The Word was in God's presence, and what God was, the Word was. John 1.1.

The new birth

The triune life of God must first have its birth in us before we can enter into the triune, beatific life or presence of God. The triune nature of the deity is that which wants to be born in us. Our redemption consists in nothing else but in the bringing forth this new birth in us, and that, being thus born again in the likeness of the Holy Trinity, we may be capable of its threefold blessing and happiness.

The holy threefold life of the Deity must stand within us, in the birth of our own life, as it does without us, so that we may be capable of living in God, and God in us. Every created thing does, must and can only want, seek, unite with and enjoy that outwardly, which is of the same nature with itself. No being can rise higher than its own life reaches.

What can be so glorious, so edifying, so ravishing, as this knowledge of God and ourselves? The very thought of our standing in this likeness and relation to the infinite Creator and Being of all beings is enough to kindle the divine life within us, and melt us into continual love and adoration. When we thus know the Holy Trinity in ourselves, and adore its high original in the Deity, we are possessed of a truth of the greatest moment that enlightens the mind.

You are light for all the world. A town that stands on a hill cannot be hidden. Matthew 5.14.

Real desire

How shall this great work, the birth of Christ, be effected in me? It might rather be said, since Christ has an infinite power, and also an infinite desire to save mankind, how can any one miss of this salvation but through his own unwillingness to be saved by him?

How was it that the lame and blind, the lunatic and leper, the publican and sinner, found Christ to be their Saviour, and to do all that for them which they wanted to be done to them? It was because they had a real desire of having that which they asked for. Therefore in true faith and prayer they applied to Christ, that his spirit and power might enter into them, and heal that which they wanted and desired to be healed in them.

Each said in faith and desire 'Lord, if You will, You can make me whole.' And the answer was always this, 'According to your faith, so be it done unto you'. This is Christ's answer now; as our faith is, so is it done unto us. And here lies the whole reason of our falling short of the salvation of Christ; because we have no will to it.

Again I tell you: if two of you agree on earth about any request you have to make, that request will be granted by my heavenly Father. For where two or three meet together in my name, I am there among them.
Matthew 18.19–20.

The discovery of ourselves

So far as we, by true resignation to God, die to the element of selfishness and our own will, so far as by universal love we die to envy, so far as by humility we die to pride, so far as by meekness we die to anger, so far we get away from the devil, enter into another kingdom and leave him to dwell without us in his own elements.

The greatest good that any man can do to himself is to give leave to this inner deformity to show itself, and not to strive by any art or management, either of negligence or amusement, to conceal it from him.

The root of a dark fire-life within us, which is of the nature of hell, with all its elements of selfishness, envy, pride and anger, must be in some way uncovered by us, and felt by us, before we can feel and groan enough under the weight of our disorder.

Repentance is but a kind of table-talk until we see so much of the deformity of our inner nature as to be in some degree frightened and terrified at the sight of it.

There must be some kind of earthquake within us, something that must rend and shake us to the bottom, before we can be aware enough either of the state of death we are in, or desirous enough of that Saviour who alone can raise us from it.

'Let be then; learn that I am God, exalted among the nations, exalted in the earth.' The Lord of Hosts is with us; the God of Jacob is our fortress. Psalm 46.10–11.

Hearsay-religion and true faith

The reason why we know so little of Jesus Christ as our Saviour, why we are so destitute of that faith in him which alone can change, rectify and redeem our souls, why we live starving in the coldness and deadness of a formal, historical hearsay-religion, is this: we are strangers to our own inner misery and wants, we know not that we lie in the jaws of death and hell.

We keep all things quiet within us, partly by outward forms and modes of religion and morality, and partly by the comforts, cares and delights of this world. Hence it is that we believe in a Saviour not because we feel an absolute want of one, but because we have been told there is one, and that it would be a rebellion against God to reject him.

True faith is a coming to Jesus Christ to be saved and delivered from a sinful nature, as the Canaanitish woman came to him and would not be denied. It is a faith that in love and longing and hunger and thirst and full assurance will lay hold on Christ as its loving, assured, certain and infallible Saviour.

It is this faith that breaks off all the bars and chains of death and hell in the soul; it is to this faith that Christ always says what he said in the gospel: 'Your faith has saved you, your sins are forgiven you; go in peace.'

He called a child, set him in front of them, and said, 'Truly I tell you: unless you turn round and become like children, you will never enter the kingdom of Heaven.' Matthew 18.2–3.

True inability

Nature must become a torment and burden to itself before it can willingly give itself up to that death through which alone it can pass into life. There is no true and real conversion, whether it be from infidelity or any other life of sin, until a man comes to know and feel that nothing less than his whole nature is to be parted with, and yet finds in himself no possibility of doing it.

This is the inability that can bring us at last to say with the apostle, 'When I am weak, then am I strong.' This is the distress that stands near to the Gate of Life. This is the despair by which we lose all our own life, to find a new one in God.

Happy therefore is it for your friend that he is come thus far, that everything is taken from him on which he trusted and found content in himself. In this state one sigh or look, or the least turning of his heart to God for help, would be the beginning of his salvation.

Job answered the Lord: 'I know you can do all things and that no purpose is beyond you. You ask: Who is this obscuring counsel yet lacking knowledge? But I have spoken of things which I have not understood, things too wonderful for me to know.' Job 42.1–3.

Your distressed state

Now, I will suppose your distressed state to be as you represent it: inwardly, darkness, heaviness, and confusion of thoughts and passions; outwardly, ill usage from friends, relations and all the world, unable to strike up the least spark of light or comfort by any thought or reasoning of your own . . .

Only let your present and past distress make you feel and acknowledge this twofold great truth: first, that in and of yourself you are nothing but darkness, vanity and misery; secondly, that of yourself you can no more help yourself to light and comfort than you can create an angel.

People at all times can assent to these two truths, but then it is an assent that has no depth or reality and so is of little or no use. But your condition has opened your heart for a deep and full conviction of these truths. Now, give way I beseech you to this conviction, and hold these two truths in the same degree of certainty as you know two and two to be four, and then you are, with the Prodigal Son, come to yourself and above half your work is done.

Being in full possession of these two truths, feeling them in the same degree of certainty as you feel your own existence, you are, under this sensibility, to give up yourself absolutely and entirely to God in Christ Jesus as into the hands of infinite Love, firmly believing this great and infallible truth, that God has no will towards you but that of infinite Love and infinite desire to make you a partaker of his divine nature. And that it is as absolutely impossible for the Father of our Lord Jesus Christ to refuse all good and life and salvation which you want, as it is for you to take it by your own power.

These are the words of the Lord God, the Holy One of Israel:
In calm detachment lies your safety, your strength in quiet trust.
Isaiah 30.15.

The flinty rock

Salvation is a birth of life, but reason can no more bring forth this birth than it can kindle life in a plant or animal. You might as well write the word flame upon the outside of a flint, and then expect that its imprisoned fire should be kindled by it, as to imagine that any images or ideal speculations of reason painted in your brain should raise your soul out of its state of death and kindle the divine life in it.

No! Would you have fire from a flint, its house of death must be shaken and its chains of darkness broken off by the strokes of a steel upon it. This must of all necessity be done to your soul; its imprisoned fire must be awakened by the sharp strokes of a steel, or no true light of life can arise in it.

O heavenly Father, touch and penetrate and shake and awaken the inmost depth and centre of my soul, that all that is within me may cry and call to you. Strike the flinty rock of my heart that the water of eternal life may spring up in it. Oh break open the gates of the great deep in my soul that your light may shine in upon me, that I may enter into your Kingdom of light and love and in your light see light.

When the Lord called him for the third time, he again went to Eli and said, 'Here I am! You did call me.' Then Eli understood that it was the Lord calling the boy; he told Samuel to go and lie down and said, 'If someone calls once more, say, "Speak, Lord; your servant is listening." ' 1 Samuel 3.8–9.

Dying to self

The one true way of dying to self is most simple and plain, it wants no arts or methods, no cells, monasteries or pilgrimages, it is equally practicable by every body, it is always at hand, it meets you in everything, it is free from all deceit, and it is never without success.

If you ask what is this one true, simple, plain, immediate and unerring way, it is the way of patience, meekness, humility and resignation to God. This is the truth and perfection of dying to self . . .

For to seek to be saved by patience, meekness, humility of heart, and resignation to God is truly coming to God through Christ; and when these tempers live and abide in you as the spirit and aim of your life, then Christ is in you of a truth and the life that you lead is not yours, but it is Christ that lives in you. For this is following Christ with all your power. You cannot possibly make more haste after him, you have no other way of walking as he walked or depending on him, but by wholly giving up yourself to that which he was, viz.; to patience, meekness, humility and resignation to God.

There are three things that last for ever: faith, hope, and love; and the greatest of the three is love. 1 Corinthians 13.13.

God must do all

Consider only this, that to be angry at our own anger, to be ashamed of our own pride and strongly resolve not to be weak, is the upshot of all human endeavours, and yet all this is rather the life than the death of self.

There is no help but from a total despair of all human help. When a man is brought to such an inner, full conviction as to have no more hope from all human means than he hopes to see with his hands or hear with his feet, then it is that he is truly prepared to die to self.

For God must do all, or all is nothing; but God cannot do all, till all is expected from him; and all is not expected from him till by a true and good despair of every human help, we have no hope, or trust, or longing after anything but a patient, meek, humble, total resignation to God.

If you are angry, do not be led into sin; do not let sunset find you
nursing your anger; and give no foothold to the devil.
Ephesians 4.26–7.

The anger is in us

There is no anger that stands between God and us but what is awakened in the dark fire of our own fallen nature. To quench this anger, and not his own, God gave his only begotten Son to be made man.

God has no more anger in himself now than he had before the creation, when he had only himself to love. The precious blood of his Son was not poured out to pacify himself (who in himself had no nature towards man but love), but it was poured out to quench the anger and fire of the fallen soul, and to kindle in it a birth of light and love.

As man lives and moves and has his being in the divine nature, and is supported by it, whether his nature be good or bad, so the anger of man, which was awakened in the dark fire of his fallen nature, may, in a certain sense, be called the anger of God, as hell itself may be said to be in God because nothing can be out of his immensity.

Yet this hell is not God. And this anger which may be called the anger of God is not God, but the fiery anger of the fallen soul.

As a father has compassion on his children, so the Lord has compassion on those who fear him; for he knows how we were made, he remembers that we are but dust. Psalm 103.13–14.

No anger in God

They who suppose the anger of God upon fallen man, to be a state of mind in God himself, to be a political kind of just indignation – a point of honourable resentment, which the sovereign deity, as governor of the world, ought not to recede from, but must have a sufficient satisfaction done to his offended authority, before he can, consistently with his sovereign honour, receive the sinner into his favour – hold the doctrine of the necessity of Christ's atoning life and death in a mistaken sense.

Neither reason nor Scripture will allow us to bring anger into God himself, as a temper of his mind, who is only infinite, unalterable, overflowing love, as unchangeable in love, as he is in power and goodness.

The anger that was awakened at the fall of man, that then seized upon him as its captive, was only a plague, or evil, or curse that sin had brought forth in nature and creature. It was only the beginning of hell. It was such an anger as God himself pitied man's lying under it. It was such an anger as God himself furnished man with a power of overcoming and extinguishing, and therefore it was not an anger that was according to the mind, will, and liking or wisdom of God. So it was not an anger that was in God himself, or which was exercised by his sovereign wisdom over his disobedient creatures.

It was such an anger as God himself hated, as he hates sin and hell. An anger that the God of all nature and creature so willed to be removed and extinguished, that seeing nothing less could do it, he sent his only begotten Son into the world, that all mankind might be saved and delivered from it.

I am the Lord; for my own sake I wipe out your transgressions and remember your sins no more. Isaiah 43.25.

God – a consuming fire

God is said to be a consuming fire. But to whom? To the fallen angels and lost souls. But why and how is he so to them? It is because those creatures have lost all that they had from God but the fire of their nature, and therefore God can only be found and manifested in them as a consuming fire.

Though God be nothing but love, yet they are under the anger and vengeance of God because they have only that fire in them which is broken off from the light and love of God, and so can know or feel nothing of God but his fire of nature in them. And yet it is still strictly true that there is no anger in God himself. He has not changed in his temper towards the creation. He does not cease to be one and the same infinite fountain of goodness, infinitely flowing forth in the riches of his love upon all and every life.

God is not changed from love to anger, but the creatures have changed their own state in nature, and so the God of nature can only be manifested in them according to their own state in nature.

It is a terrifying thing to fall into the hands of the living God.
Hebrews 10.31.

The innocent Christ

The innocent Christ did not suffer to quiet an angry deity, but merely as co-operating, assisting and uniting with that love of God which desired our salvation.

He did not suffer in our place or stead, but only on our account, which is a quite different matter. And to say that he suffered in our place and stead is as absurd, as contrary to Scripture, as to say that he rose from the dead and ascended into heaven in our place and stead, that we might be excused from it.

For his sufferings, death, resurrection and ascension are all of them equally on our account, for our sake, for our good and benefit, but none of them possible to be in our stead.

We know that our old humanity has been crucified with Christ, for the destruction of the sinful self, so that we may no longer be slaves to sin, because death cancels the claims of sin. Romans 6.6–7.

The inner new man

All our salvation consists in the manifestation of the nature, life and spirit of Jesus Christ in our inner new man. This alone is Christian redemption, this alone delivers from the guilt and power of sin. This alone redeems, renews and regains the first life of God in the soul of man. Everything besides this is self, is fiction, is propriety, is self-will, and however coloured is only your old man, with all his deeds.

Enter therefore with all your heart into this truth. Let your eye be always upon it, do everything in view of it, try everything by the truth of it, love nothing but for the sake of it. Wherever you go, whatever you do, at home or abroad, in the field or at church, do all in a desire of union with Christ, in imitation of his tempers and inclinations, and look upon all as nothing but that which exercises and increases the spirit and life of Christ in your soul ...

When God has all that he should have of your heart, when renouncing the will, judgement, tempers and inclinations of the old man, you are wholly given up to the obedience of the light and spirit of God within you, to will only his holy will, to love only in his love, to be wise only in his wisdom, then it is that everything that you do is as a song of praise, and the common business of your life is a conforming to God's will on earth, as angels do in heaven.

For all alike have sinned, and are deprived of the divine glory; and all are justified by God's free grace alone, through his act of liberation in the person of Christ Jesus. Romans 3.23–4.

Christ in us the hope of glory

A Christ not in us is the same thing as a Christ not ours. If we are only so far with Christ as to own and receive the history of his birth, person and character, if this is all that we have of him, we are as much without him, as much left to ourselves, as little helped by him as those evil spirits which cried out 'we know you, who you are, you holy one of God'.

It is the language of Scripture that Christ in us is our hope of glory, that Christ formed in us, growing and raising his own life and spirit in us, is our only salvation. Since the serpent, sin, death and hell are all essentially within us – the very growth of our nature – must not our redemption be equally inward, an inner essential death to this state of our souls, and an inner growth of a contrary life within us?

For it is in Christ that the Godhead in all its fullness dwells embodied, it is in him you have been brought to fulfilment. Every power and authority in the universe is subject to him as head.
Colossians 2.9–10.

The book of the heart

The book of all books is in your own heart, in which are written and engraved the deepest lessons of divine instruction. Learn therefore to be deeply attentive to the presence of God in your heart, who is always speaking, always instructing, always illuminating the heart that is attentive to him.

Here you will meet the divine light in its proper place, in that depth of your soul, where the birth of the Son of God and the proceeding of the Holy Ghost are always ready to spring up in you.

And be assured of this, that so much as you have of inward love and adherence to his holy light and spirit within you, so much as you have of real unaffected humility and meekness, so much as you are dead to your own will and self-love, so much as you have of purity of heart, so much and no more, nor any further, do you see and know the truths of God.

For anyone united to Christ, there is a new creation: the old order has gone; a new order has already begun. 2 Corinthians 5.17.

What we mean by the heart

We mean by *the heart* that it is a kind of life and motion within us which everyone knows contains all that is good or bad in us; that we are what our hearts are. This state of our heart is as distinct from and independent of all speculations of our reasoning faculties as it is distinct from and independent of all the languages in which a scholar can reason and speculate about it.

Our heart is our manner of existence, or the state in which we feel ourselves to be. It is an inward life, a vital sensibility which contains our manner of feeling what and how we are. It is the state of our desires and tendencies, of inwardly seeing, hearing, tasting, relishing and feeling that which passes within us. It is to us inwardly with regard to ourselves what our senses of seeing, hearing, feeling, etc., are with regard to things that are external to us ...

It is the sensibility of the soul that must receive what the world communicates to it. It is the sensibility of the soul that must receive what God can communicate to it. Reason may follow after in either case and view through its own glass what is done, but it can do no more.

I shall give them singleness of heart and put a new spirit in them; I shall remove the heart of stone from their bodies and give them a heart of flesh, so that they will conform to my statutes and keep my laws.
Ezekiel 11.19–20.

A true and false desire

Do not all Christians desire to have Christ to be their Saviour? Yes. But here is the deceit; all would have Christ to be their Saviour in the next world and to help them into heaven when they die, by his power and merits with God.

But this is not willing Christ to be your Saviour; for his salvation, if it is to be had, must be had in this world. If he saves you it must be done in this life by changing all that is within you, by helping you to a new heart, as he helped the blind to see, the lame to walk and the dumb to speak.

For to have salvation from Christ is nothing else but to be made like him. It is to have his humility and meekness, his mortification and self-denial, his renunciation of the spirit, wisdom and honours of this world, his love of God, his desire of doing God's will and seeking only his honour.

To have these tempers formed and begotten in your heart is to have salvation from Christ. If you will not to have these tempers brought out in you, if your faith and desire does not seek and cry to Christ for them in the same reality as the lame asked to walk and the blind to see, then you must be said to be unwilling to have Christ to be your Saviour.

I have been crucified with Christ; the life I now live is not my life, but the life which Christ lives in me. Galatians 2.20.

The soul's food

Nothing does or can keep God out of the soul but the desire of the heart turned from him. And the reason for it is this: it is because the life of the soul is in itself nothing but a working will; and therefore wherever the will works or goes, there and there only the soul lives, whether it be in God or the creature.

Whatever it desires, that is the fuel of its fire; and as its fuel is, so is the flame of its life. A will given up to earthly goods has one life with the beasts of the field. Wherever and in whatever the working will chooses to dwell and delight, that becomes the soul's food, its condition, its body, its clothing and habitation.

Is there anything so frightful as this worldly spirit which turns the soul from God, makes it a house of darkness and feeds it with the food of time? On the other hand, what can be so desirable as the spirit of prayer which empties the soul of all its own evil, separates death and darkness from it, leaves self, time and the world, and becomes one life with Christ?

Whoever eats my flesh and drinks my blood has eternal life, and I will raise him up on the last day. John 6.54.

The work of repentance

All depends upon your right submission and obedience to the speaking of God in your soul. Stop therefore all self-activity. Listen not to the suggestions of your own reason, run not on in your own will. Be retired, silent, passive and humbly attentive to this new risen light within you.

Open your heart, your eyes and ears, to all its impressions. Let it enlighten, teach, frighten, torment, judge and condemn you as it pleases. Turn not away from it, hear all it says, seek for no relief out of it, consult not with flesh and blood. With a heart full of faith and resignation to God, pray only this prayer, that God's Kingdom may come and his will be done in your soul.

Stand faithfully in this state of preparation, thus given up to the spirit of God, and then the work of your repentance will be wrought in God. You will soon find that he that is in you is much greater than all that are against you.

But Zacchaeus stood there and said to the Lord, 'Here and now, sir, I give half my possessions to charity; and if I have defrauded anyone, I will repay him four times over.' Jesus said to him, 'Today salvation has come to this house – for this man too is a son of Abraham.'
Luke 19.8–9.

Self-denials

As to the nature of our self-denials and mortifications, considered in themselves they have nothing of goodness or holiness. Nor are they any real parts of our sanctification. They are not the true food or nourishment of the divine life in our souls. They have no quickening, sanctifying power in them.

Their only worth is that they remove the impediments of holiness, break down that which stands between God and us, and make way for the quickening, sanctifying spirit of God to operate on our souls. Which operation of God is the one only thing that can raise the divine life in the soul, or help it to the smallest degree of real holiness or spiritual life.

All human work of self-denial has no good in itself, but is only to open an entrance for the one only good, the light of God, to operate upon us.

I may give all I possess to the needy, I may give my body to be burnt, but if I have no love, I gain nothing by it. 1 Corinthians 13.3.

Nothing is in vain to the humble soul

Nothing is in vain or without profit to the humble soul; like the bee it takes its honey even from bitter herbs. It stands always in a state of divine growth, and everything that falls upon it is like the dew of heaven to it.

Shut up yourself therefore in this form of humility, all good is enclosed in it. It is a water of heaven that turns the fire of the fallen soul into the meekness of the divine life. Let it be as a garment with which you are always covered, and the girdle which you put around you.

Breathe nothing but in and from its spirit. See nothing but with its eyes; hear nothing but with its ears. And then, whether you are in the church or out of the church, hearing the praises of God or receiving wrongs from men and the world, everything will help forward your growth in the life of God.

When you receive an invitation, go and sit down in the lowest place, so that when your host comes he will say, 'Come up higher, my friend.'
Luke 14.10.

Religious zeal

Would you know whence it is that so many false spirits have appeared in the world who have deceived themselves and others with false fire and false light, laying claim to inspirations, illuminations and openings of the divine life, pretending to do wonders under extraordinary calls from God? It is this; they have turned to God without turning from themselves. They would be alive in God before they were dead to their own nature; a thing impossible as for a grain of wheat to be alive before it dies.

Now religion in the hands of self or corrupt nature serves only to discover vices of a worse kind than nature left to itself. Hence all the disorderly passions of religious men: pride, self-exaltation, hatred and persecution – which burn a worse flame than passions only employed about worldly matters – are under a cloak of religious zeal, and will sanctify actions which nature left to itself, would be ashamed to own.

Be on the alert! Wake up! Your enemy the devil, like a roaring lion, prowls around looking for someone to devour. Stand up to him, firm in your faith. 1 Peter 5.8–9.

Turning to God

Turning to God according to the inner feeling, want and motion of your own heart, in love, in trust, in faith of having from him all that you want to have, this turning thus unto God, whether it be with or without words, is the best form of prayer in the world.

Now no man can be ignorant of the state of his own heart or a stranger to those tempers that are alive and stirring in him. Therefore no man can lack a form of prayer; for what should be the form of his prayer but the condition and state his heart demands?

Prayers not formed according to the real state of your heart are only like a prayer to be pulled out of a deep well when you are not in it. Hence you may see how unreasonable it is to make a mystery of prayer, or an art that needs so much instruction; since every man is, and only can be, directed by his own inner state and condition when and how and what he is to pray.

We do not even know how we ought to pray, but through our inarticulate groans the Spirit himself is pleading for us.
Romans 8.26.

A continual state of prayer

Every man's life is a continual state of prayer. He is no moment free from it, nor can possibly be so.

All our natural tempers, be they what they will, ambition, covetousness, selfishness, worldly-mindedness, pride, envy, hatred, malice or any other lust whatever, are all of them in reality only so many different kinds and forms of a spirit of prayer which is inseparable from the heart as weight is from the body.

Every natural temper is nothing else but a manifestation of the desire and prayer of the heart, and shows us how it works and wills. And as the heart works and wills, such and no other is its prayer.

If therefore the working desire of the heart is not habitually turned towards God, if this is not our spirit of prayer, we are necessarily in a state of prayer towards something else that carries us from God and brings all kind of evil into us. Pray we must, as sure as our heart is alive; and therefore when the state of our heart is not a spirit of prayer to God, we pray without ceasing to some or other part of the creation.

Enter in! Let us bow down in worship, let us kneel before the Lord who made us, for he is our God, we are the people he shepherds, the flock in his care. Psalm 95.6–7.

Imaginations and desires

We are apt to think that our imaginations and desires may be played with, that they rise and fall away as nothing, because they do not always bring forth outward and visible effects. But in fact they are the greatest reality we have, and are the true formers and raisers of all that is real and solid in us. All outward power that we exercise in the things about us, is but as a shadow in comparison of that inner power, that resides in our will, imagination and desires; these communicate with eternity.

They kindle a life which always reaches either heaven or hell. This strength of the inner man makes all that is the angel, and all that is the devil in us. We are neither good nor bad, but according to the working of that which is spiritual and invisible in us. Now our desire is not only thus powerful and productive of real effects, but it is always alive, always working and creating in us. Creating – for it has no less power – it perpetually generates either life or death in us. And here lies the ground of the great efficacy of prayer, which when it is the prayer of the heart, the prayer of faith, has a kindling and a creating power, and forms and transforms the soul into every thing that its desires reach after.

It has the key to the Kingdom of heaven, and unlocks all its treasures, it opens, extends and moves that in us, which has its being and motion in and with the divine nature, and so brings us into a real union and communion with God.

For our struggle is not against human foes, but against cosmic powers, against the authorities and potentates of this dark age, against the superhuman forces of evil in the heavenly realms. Ephesians 6.12.

A method of prayer

The best help you can have from a book is to read one full of such truths, instructions and awakening informations as force you to see and know who and what and where you are; that God is your All; and that all is misery but a heart and life devoted to him. This is the best outward prayer book you can have, as it will turn you to an inner book and spirit of prayer in your heart.

When for the sake of this inner prayer you retire at any time of the day, never begin until you know and feel why and wherefore you are going to pray. Let this why and wherefore form and direct everything that comes from you whether it be in thought or word.

No good desire can languish when once your heart is in this method of prayer; never beginning to pray until you first see how matters stand with you; asking your heart what it wants, and having nothing in your prayers but what the known state of your heart puts you to demanding, saying or offering unto God. Thus praying you can never pray in vain.

Moses prayed, 'Show me your glory.' The Lord answered, 'I shall make all my goodness pass before you, and I shall pronounce in your hearing the name "Lord". I shall be gracious to whom I shall be gracious, and I shall have compassion on whom I shall have compassion.' But he added, 'My face you cannot see, for no mortal may see me and live.' Exodus 33.18–20.

Different forms of prayer

Every man that has any feeling of the weight of his sin, or any true desire to be delivered from it by Christ, has learning and capacity enough to make his own prayer. Praying is not speaking out eloquently, but simply the true desire of the heart.

The most simple souls that have accustomed themselves to speak their own desires and wants to God, in such short but true breathings of their hearts to him, will soon know more of prayer and the mysteries of it than any persons who have their knowledge only from learning and learned books.

It is not silence, or a simple petition, or a great variety of outward expressions that alters the nature of prayer, or makes it good or better, but only and solely the reality, steadiness and continuity of the desire. Whether a man offers this desire to God in the silent longing of the heart, or in simple short petitions, or in a great variety of words is of no consequence. But if you would know what I would call a true and great gift of prayer, and what I most of all wish for myself, it is a good heart that stands continually inclined towards God.

But when you pray, go into a room by yourself, shut the door, and pray to your Father who is in secret; and your Father who sees what is done in secret will reward you. Matthew 6.6.

The natural language of the heart

The best instruction that I can give you as helpful or preparatory to the spirit of prayer is already fully given, where we have set forth the original perfection, the miserable fall, and the glorious redemption of man. These things must fill you with a dislike of your present state, drive all earthly desires out of your soul, and create an earnest longing after your first perfection.

Prayer cannot be taught you by giving you a book of prayers, but by awakening in you a true sense and knowledge of what you are and what you should be. Man does not, cannot, pray for anything because a fine petition for it is put into his hands, but because his own condition is a reason and motive for his asking for it.

It cannot be wrong or hurtful to any body to show that prayer is the natural language of the heart, and, as such, does not want any form of borrowed words. Now, all that has been said of manuals of prayers only amounts to thus much, that they are not necessary, nor the most natural and excellent way of praying. If they happen to be necessary to any person, or to be his most excellent way, it is because the natural real prayer of his heart is already engaged, loving, wishing, and longing after the things of this life, which makes him so insensible of his spiritual wants, so blind and dead as to the things of God, that he cannot pray for them except so far as the words of other people are put into his mouth.

If a man is blind and knows it not, he may be told to pray for sight. If he is sick and knows nothing of it, he may be told to pray for health; so, if the soul is in this state with regard to its spiritual wants, a manual may be of good use to it, not so much by helping it to pray, as by showing it at what a miserable distance it is from those tempers which belong to prayer.

Ask, and you will receive; seek, and you will find; knock and the door will be opened to you. Matthew 7.7.

The true desire of the heart

When a man has had so much benefit from the gospel as to know his own misery, his want of a Redeemer, who he is, and how he is to be found, there everything seems to be done, both to awaken and direct his prayer and make it a true praying in and by the Spirit. When the heart really pants and longs after God, its prayer is a praying as moved and animated by the spirit of God; it is the breath or inspiration of God, stirring, moving and opening itself in the heart.

Nothing in the heart can pray, aspire, and long after God without the Spirit of God moving and stirring in it. Every breath, therefore, of the true spirit of prayer can be nothing else but the breath of the Spirit of God, breathing, inspiring and moving the heart in all its variety of motions and affections towards God.

Every time a good desire stirs in the heart, a good prayer goes out of it that reaches God as being the fruit and work of his Holy Spirit. When any man, feeling his corruption and the power of sin in his soul, looks up to God with true earnestness of faith and desire to be delivered from it, whether with words or without words, how can he pray better?

It is the reality, the steadiness and continuity of the desire that is the goodness of prayer and its qualification to receive all that it wants. For praying is not speaking forth eloquently, but simply the true desire of the heart; and the heart, simple and plain in good desires, is in the truest state of preparation for all the gifts and graces of God.

For a long time she went on praying before the Lord, while Eli watched her lips. Hannah was praying silently; her lips were moving, although her voice could not be heard, and Eli took her for a drunken woman. 1 Samuel 1.12–13.

Prayers

O God, in whom nothing can live but as it lives in love, grant us the spirit of love which does not want to be rewarded, honoured or esteemed, but only to become the blessing and happiness of everything that wants it; which is the very joy of life, and your own goodness and truth in our soul; who yourself are love, and by love our Redeemer, from eternity to eternity.   Amen.

O heavenly Father, infinite, fathomless depth of never-ceasing Love, save me from myself, from the disorderly workings of my fallen, long corrupted nature, and let my eyes see, my heart and spirit feel and find, your salvation in Christ Jesus.

O God, who made me for yourself, to show forth your goodness in me, manifest, I humbly beseech you, the life-giving power of your holy nature within me; help me to such a true and living faith in you, such strength of hunger and thirst after the birth, life and spirit of your holy Jesus in my soul, that all that is within me, may be turned from every inner thought, or outward work, that is not you, your holy Jesus, and heavenly working in my soul.   Amen.

Pray continually; give thanks whatever happens; for this is what God wills for you in Christ Jesus. 1 Thessalonians 5.17–18.

Practice and Salvation

The pearl of eternity

This pearl of eternity is the Church or Temple of God within you, the consecrated place of divine worship, where alone you can worship God in spirit and in truth. In spirit, because your spirit is that alone in you, which can unite and cleave unto God and receive the workings of his divine Spirit upon you. In truth, because this adoration in spirit is that truth and reality, of which all outward forms and rites, though instituted by God, are only the figure for a time; but this worship is eternal. Accustom yourself to the holy service of this inner temple. There the mysteries of your redemption are celebrated, or rather opened in life and power. There the Supper of the Lamb is kept; the bread that came down from Heaven, that gives life to the world, is your true nourishment: all is done and known in real experience, in a living sensibility of the work of God on the soul. There the birth, the life, the sufferings, the death, the resurrection and ascension of Christ are not merely remembered, but inwardly found and enjoyed as the real states of your soul, which has followed Christ in the regeneration. When once you are well grounded in this inner worship, you will have learnt to live unto God above time and place. For every day will be Sunday to you, and wherever you go you will have a priest, a church and an altar along with you. For when renouncing the will, judgement, tempers and inclinations of your old man, you are wholly given up to the obedience of the light and Spirit of God within you, to will only in his will, to love only in his love, then it is that everything you do is as a song of praise, and the common business of your life is a conforming to God's will on earth as angels do in Heaven.

Lord, you have been our refuge throughout all generations. Before the mountains were brought forth or the earth and the world were born, from age to age you are God. Psalm 90.1–2.

The natural state of our tempers

The natural state of our tempers has a variety of covers, under which they lie concealed at times, both from ourselves and others. When this or that accident happens to displace such a cover, then that which lay hidden under it breaks out. And then we vainly think that this or that outward occasion has not shown us how we are within, but has only infused or put into us an anger, or grief, or envy which is not our natural state, or of our own growth.

But this is mere blindness and self-deceit, for it is as impossible for the mind to have any grief, anger or joy except what it has all from its own inner state, as for the instrument to give forth any other harmony or discord but that which is within and from itself.

Persons, things and occurrences may strike our instrument improperly and variously, but as we are in ourselves, such is our outward sound, whatever strikes us. If our inner state is the renewed life of Christ within us, then every thing and occasion, let it be what it will, only makes the same life to sound out and show itself.

Peter said, 'Even if I have to die with you, I will never disown you.'
And all the disciples said the same. Matthew 26.35.

Christ given into us

Christ given for us is neither more nor less than Christ given into us. He is in no other sense our full, perfect and sufficient atonement than as his nature and spirit are born and formed in us, which so purge us from our sins that we are thereby in him, and by him dwelling in us, become new creatures, having our conversation in heaven.

As Adam is truly our defilement and impurity, by his birth in us, so Christ is our atonement and purification, by our being born again of him, and having thereby quickened and revived in us that first divine life which was extinguished in Adam.

And therefore, as Adam purchased death for us, just so in the same manner, in the same degree, and in the same sense, Christ purchases life for us. And each of them solely by their own inner life in us.

If you dwell in me, and my words dwell in you, ask whatever you want, and you shall have it. John 15.7.

Election and reprobation

Nothing is elected, foreseen, predestinated or called according to the purpose of God except this seed of the new man, because the one eternal, unchangeable purpose of God towards man is only this, namely that man should be a heavenly image or son of God.

On the other hand, nothing is reprobated, rejected or cast out by God except the earthly nature which came from the fall of Adam. This is the only vessel of anger, the son of perdition, that can have no share in the promises and blessings of God.

Here you have the whole unalterable ground of divine election and reprobation. It relates not to any particular number of people or division of mankind, but solely to the two natures that are, both of them, without exception, in every individual of mankind. All that is earthly, serpentine and devilish in every man is reprobated and doomed to destruction; and the heavenly seed of new birth in every man is that which is chosen, ordained and called to eternal life.

Election therefore and reprobation, as respecting salvation, relate equally to every man in the world; because every man has that in him which only is elected, and that in him which only is reprobated, namely the heavenly seed of the Word of God and the earthly nature.

Integrity is a guide for the upright; the perfidious are ruined by their own duplicity. Proverbs 11.3.

Your heart as a den of thieves

You will perhaps say it is your very heart that keeps you a stranger to Christ and him to you, because your heart is all bad, as unholy as a den of thieves.

I answer that the finding this to be the state of your heart is the real finding of Christ in it. For nothing else but Christ can reveal and make manifest the sin and evil in you. And he that discloses is the same Christ that takes away sin. So that as soon as complaining guilt sets itself before you and will be seen, you may be assured that Christ is in you of a truth.

Christ must first come as a discloser and reprover of sin. It is the infallible proof of his holy presence within you. Hear him, reverence him, submit to him as a discloser and reprover of sin.

Own his power and his presence in the feeling of your guilt and then he that wounded will heal, he that found out the sin will take it away, and he that showed you your den of thieves will turn it into a holy temple of Father, Son and Holy Ghost.

Alas for you, scribes and Pharisees, hypocrites! You clean the outside of a cup or a dish, and leave the inside full of greed and self-indulgence! Blind Pharisee! Clean the inside of the cup first; then the outside will be clean also. Matthew 23.25–6.

The way of the returning prodigal

Jacob Boehme absolutely requires his reader to be in the way of the returning prodigal. It is not rules of morality observed or an outward blameless form of life that will do. Pride, vanity, envy, self-love and love of the world can be, and often are, the heart of such a morality of life. But the state of the lost son is quite another thing.

As soon as he comes to himself and has seeing eyes, he will then, like him, see himself far from home; that he has lost his first paradise, his heavenly Father, and the dignity of his first birth; that he is a poor, beggarly slave in a foreign land, hungry, ragged and starving among the lowest kind of beasts, not so well fed and clothed as they are.

Wherever the gospel itself is received and professed without something of this preparation of heart, without this sensibility of the lost son, there it can only be a stumbling stone and help the earthly man to form a religion based on notions and opinions from the unfelt meaning of the letter of the gospel.

A pure and faultless religion in the sight of God the Father is this: to look after orphans and widows in trouble and to keep oneself untarnished by the world. James 1.27.

The spirit of prayer is for all times

The poverty of our fallen nature, the depraved workings of flesh and blood, the corrupt tempers of our polluted birth in this world do not hurt us so long as the spirit of prayer works contrary to them and longs for the first birth of the light and spirit of heaven.

All our natural evil ceases to be our own evil as soon as our will-spirit turns from it. It then changes its nature, loses all its poison and death, and only becomes our holy cross on which we happily die from self and this world into the kingdom of heaven.

Reading is good, hearing is good, conversation and meditation are good; but they are only good at times and occasions.

The spirit of prayer is for all times and all occasions. It is a lamp that is to be always burning, a light to be ever shining; everything calls for it, everything is to be done in it and governed by it. It is, and means and wills, nothing else except the whole totality of the soul not doing this or that, but wholly, incessantly given up to God to be where and what and how he pleases.

I love the Lord, for he has heard me and listened to my prayer; he has given me a hearing and all my days I shall cry to him.
Psalm 116.1–2.

Speech and silence

The spiritual life is nothing else but the working of the spirit of God within us, and therefore our own silence must be a great part of our preparation for it, and much speaking or delight in it will be often no small hindrance of that good which we can only have from hearing what the spirit and voice of God speaks within us.

This is not enough known by religious persons. They rejoice in kindling a fire of their own, and delight too much in hearing of their own voice, and so lose that inner unction from above which can alone newly create their hearts.

To speak with the tongues of men or angels on religious matters is a much less thing than to know how to stay the mind upon God, and abide with him in the closet of our hearts, observing, loving, adoring and obeying his holy power within us.

I have written very largely on the spiritual life, and he understands not my writings, nor the end of them, who does not see that their whole drift is to call all Christians to a God and Christ within them as the only possible life, light and power of all goodness they can ever have. I invite all people to the marriage of the Lamb, but no one to myself.

Now when the Lamb broke the seventh seal, there was silence in heaven for about half an hour. Revelation 8.1.

The one will of love

As love has no by-ends, wills nothing but its own increase, so everything is as oil to its flame; it must have that which it wills. It cannot be disappointed, because everything naturally helps it to live in its own way, and to bring forth its own work.

The spirit of love does not want to be rewarded, honoured or esteemed. Its only desire is to propagate itself, and become the blessing and happiness of everything that wants it. And therefore it meets anger and evil and hatred and opposition with the same one will as the light meets the darkness, only to overcome it with all its blessings.

Did you want to avoid the anger or ill-will, or to gain the favour of any persons, you might easily miss your goal. But if you have no will but to all goodness, everything you meet, be it what it will, must be forced to be of assistance to you. For the anger of an enemy, the treachery of a friend, and every other evil only help the spirit of love to be more triumphant, to live its own life, and find all its own blessings in a higher degree.

Love is patient and kind. Love envies no one, is never boastful, never conceited, never rude; love is never selfish, never quick to take offence.
1 Corinthians 13.4–5.

Inner and outward religion

He that thinks or holds that outward exercises of religion hurt or are too low for his degree of spirituality shows plainly that his spirituality is only in idea.

The truly spiritual man is he that sees God in all things and all things in God. Every outward thing has the nature of a sacrament to him.

To such a one the outward institutions of religion are ten times more dear and valuable than to those that are less spiritual. As the truly charitable man loves to meet outward objects of charity, as the truly humble man loves to meet outward occasions of being abased, so the truly spiritual man loves all outward objects and institutions that can exercise the religion of the heart.

And to think that the spirituality of religion is hurt by the observance of outward institutions of religion is as absurd as to think that the inner spirit of charity is hurt by the observance of outward acts of charity, or the spiritual joy of the heart destroyed by singing an outward hymn, as our Saviour and his apostles did.

Men of Athens, I see that in everything that concerns religion you are uncommonly scrupulous. As I was going round looking at the objects of your worship, I noticed among other things an altar bearing the inscription 'To an Unknown God'. Acts 17.22–3.

The one humility

Here it is seen that every son of Adam is in the service of pride and self, be he doing what he will, till an humility that comes solely from heaven has been his redeemer. He that thinks it possible for the natural man to get a better humility than this from his own reason, shows himself quite ignorant of this one most plain and capital truth of the gospel, namely, that there never was, nor ever will be, but one humility in the whole world, and that is the one humility of Christ, which never any man, since the fall of Adam, had the least degree of except from Christ.

Humility is one, in the same sense and truth as Christ is one, the Mediator is one, Redemption is one. If there was any humility besides that of Christ, there would be something else besides him that could take away the sins of the world. 'All that came before me,' says Christ, 'were thieves and robbers.' The same is as true of every virtue, whether it has the name of humility, charity, piety, or anything else; if it comes before Christ, however good it may pretend to be, it is but a cheat, a thief and a robber, under the name of a godly virtue. This is because pride and self have the all of man till man has his all from Christ. He therefore only fights the good fight, whose strife is that the self-idolatrous nature, which he has from Adam, may be brought to death by the supernatural humility of Christ brought to life in him. The enemies to man's rising out of the fall of Adam, through the Spirit and Power of Christ, are many. But the one great dragon-enemy, called antichrist, is SELF-EXALTATION. This is his birth, his pomp, his power and his throne; when self-exaltation ceases, the last enemy is destroyed, and all that came from the pride and death of Adam is swallowed up in victory.

Even among those in authority many believed in him, but would not acknowledge him on account of the Pharisees, for fear of being banned from the synagogue. For they valued human reputation rather than the honour which comes from God. John 12.42–3.

The patience of the Lamb of God

Turn from anger of every kind, as you would flee from the most horrid devil; for it is his, it is he, and his strength in you. Whether you look at rage and anger in a tempest, a beast, or a man, it is but one and the same thing, from one and the same cause. Your own anger is to be turned from.

This must be, till the centre of nature is again in its place of hiddenness, by being wholly overcome by heaven. Embrace, therefore, every meekness of love and humility with the same eagerness as you would fall down at the feet of Jesus Christ, for it is his, it is he, and his power of salvation in you. Enter into no strife or self-defence against any one that either reproaches you or your doctrine.

Remember that, if you are to join with Christ in doing good, your sword of natural anger must be locked up in its own sheath; no weapons of flesh are to be used. You must work only in the meekness, the sweetness, the humility, the love and patience of the Lamb of God, who, as such, is the only doer of good, the only overcomer of anger, and the one redemption of fallen nature. As in good report you are to be as though you heard it not, ascribe nothing to yourself from it; so in evil report, self is just as much to be forgotten; both are to be used only as an occasion to generate humility, meekness, love and the spirit of the Lamb of God, both in yourself and all that speak either well or ill of you. For this is the will and working of heaven; it has but one will and one work, and that is, to change all the anger, evil and disorder of nature into a Kingdom of God.

He that would be a servant of God and work with heaven must will all that he wills, do all that he does, and bear all that he bears, in the one spirit and one will with which heaven rules over all the earth.

Do not resist those who wrong you. If anyone slaps you on the right cheek, turn and offer him the other also. Matthew 5.39.

The whole of man's salvation

This salvation, which is God's mercy to the fallen soul of man merely as fallen, must be something that meets every man. Every man, as fallen, has something that directs him to turn to it. For as the fall of man is the reason of this mercy, so the fall must be the guide to it. The want must show the thing that is wanted. And, therefore, the manifestation of this one salvation or mercy to man must have a nature suitable, not to this or that great reader of history or able critic in Hebrew roots and Greek phrases, but suitable to the common state and condition of every son of Adam. It must be something as grounded in human nature as the fall itself is, which wants no art to make it known, but to which the common nature of man is the only guide in one man as well as another. Now, this something, which is thus obvious to every man, and which opens the way to redemption in every soul, is a sense of the vanity and misery of this world, and a prayer of faith and hope to God to be raised to a better state.

Now, in this sensibility, which every man's own nature leads him into, lies the whole of man's salvation. Here the mercy of God and the misery of man are met together. Here the fall and the redemption kiss each other. This is the Christianity which is as old as the fall, which alone saved the first man, and can alone save the last. This is it, on which hang all the law and the prophets, and which fulfils them both; for they have only this end, to turn man from the lusts of this life to a desire and faith and hope of a better. Thus does the whole of Christian redemption stand so near and plain to all mankind.

When Jesus saw her weeping and the Jews who had come with her weeping, he was moved with indignation and deeply distressed. 'Where have you laid him?' he asked. They replied, 'Come and see.' Jesus wept. The Jews said, 'How dearly he must have loved him!'
John 11.33–6.

Preaching

The first business of a clergyman awakened by God into a sensibility and love of the truths of the gospel, and of making them equally felt and loved by others, is thankfully, joyfully and calmly to adhere to, and give way to, the increase of this new-risen light. And by true introversion of his heart to God as the sole Author of it, humbly to beg of him that all that which he feels a desire of doing to those under his care may be first truly and fully done in himself.

Keep guard over yourselves and over all the flock of which the Holy Spirit has given you charge, as shepherds of the church of the Lord, which he won for himself by his own blood. Acts 20.28.

Self-evident

Observe the word *self-evident*, for there lies the truth of the matter. You have no more of the truth of religion than what is self-evident in you. Now, religion is light and life; but light and life can only manifest themselves, and can nowhere be known but where they are self-evident. You can know nothing of God, of nature, of heaven, or hell, or yourself, but so far as all these things are self-evident in you. Turn to that which is sensible and self-evident in you, and then you must know, in the same certainty as you know yourself to be alive, that there is anger, self-torment, envy, malice, evil-will, pride, cruelty, revenge, etc. Now, say if you please, there are no other devils but these and that men have no other devils to resist, and then you will have said the truth enough, have owned devils enough, and enough confessed that you are in the midst of them, that you are everywhere tempted by them.

If you turn from all idle debates and demonstrations of reason to that which is sensible and self-evident in you, then you have a sensible, self-evident proof of the true God of Life and Light and Love and Goodness, as manifest to you as your own life. For, with the same self-evident certainty as you know that you think and are alive, you know that there is goodness, love, benevolence, meekness, compassion, wisdom, peace, joy. Now, this is the self-evident God that forces himself to be known and found and felt in every man in the same certainty of self-evidence as every man feels and finds his own thoughts and life. This is the God whose being and providence call for our worship and love and adoration and obedience to him. And this worship and love and adoration and conformity to the divine goodness is our true belief in and sure knowledge of the self-evident God.

In those days it will no longer be said, 'Parents have eaten sour grapes and the children's teeth are set on edge'; for everyone will die for his own wrong-doing; he who eats the sour grapes will find his own teeth set on edge. Jeremiah 31.29–30.

Awareness

This is the One True God, or the Deity of goodness, virtue, love, etc., the certainty of whose being and providence opens itself to you in the self-evident sensibility of your own nature, and inspires his likeness and love of his goodness into you. As this is the only true knowledge that you can possibly have of God and the divine nature, so it is a knowledge not to be debated or lessened by any objections of reason but is as self-evident as your own life. To find or know God in reality by any outward proofs, or by anything but by God himself made manifest and self-evident in you, will never be your case either here or hereafter. For neither God, nor heaven, nor hell, nor the devil, nor the world and the flesh can be any otherwise knowable in you or by you, except by their own existence and manifestation in you. All pretended knowledge of any of these things, beyond or without this self-evident sensibility of their birth within you, is only such knowledge of them as the blind man has of that light that never entered into him. And as this is our only true knowledge, so every man is, by his birth and nature, brought into a certain and self-evident sensibility of all these things. If we bring ourselves, by reasoning and dispute, into an uncertainty about them, it is an uncertainty that we have created for ourselves, and comes not from God and nature. For God and nature have made that which is our greatest concern to be our greatest certainty, and to be known by us in the same self-evidence as our own pain or pleasure is. For nothing is religion, or the truth of religion, nothing is good or bad to you, but that which is a self-evident birth within you.

For these are the words of the Lord: As I brought upon this people all this great disaster, so shall I bring them all the prosperity which I now promise them. Fields will again be bought and sold in this land of which you now say, 'It is a desolation abandoned by man and beast; it is given over to the Chaldaeans.' Jeremiah 32.42–3.

The quickening of the Holy Spirit

See the state of man as redeemed. He has a spark of the light and Spirit of God as a supernatural gift of God given into the birth of his soul, to bring forth by degrees a new birth of that life which was lost in Paradise. This holy spark of the divine nature within him has a natural, strong, and almost infinite tendency or reaching after that eternal light and Spirit of God from whence it came forth. It came forth from God, it partakes of the divine nature, and therefore it is always in a state of return to God. All this is called the breathing, the quickening of the Holy Spirit within us, which are so many operations of this spark of life tending towards God.

On the other hand, the Deity as considered in itself and without the soul of man has an infinite, unchangeable tendency of love and desire towards the soul of man, to unite and communicate its own riches and glories to it – just as air outside man unites and communicates its riches and virtues to air that is within man. This love or desire of God towards the soul of man is so great that he gave his only begotten Son, to take human nature upon him in its fallen state, that by this mysterious union of God and man all the enemies of the soul of man might be overcome, and every human creature might have a power of being re-born.

The gospel is the history of this love of God to man. Inwardly he has a seed of the divine life given into the birth of his soul, a seed that has all the riches of eternity in it and is always wanting to come to the birth in him and be alive in God. Outwardly he has Jesus Christ, who is always casting forth his enlivening beams on this inner seed, to kindle and call it forth to birth, doing that to this seed of Heaven in man which the sun in the firmament is always doing to the vegetable seeds in the earth.

Whenever I said, 'I shall not call it to mind or speak in his name again,' then his word became imprisoned within me like a fire burning in my heart. I was weary with holding it under, and could endure no more. Jeremiah 20.9.

One salvation

There is but one salvation for all mankind, and that is the life of God in the soul. God has but one intent towards all mankind, and that is to introduce or generate his own life, light and spirit in them, that all may be as so many temples of the Holy Trinity.

This is God's will to all Christians, Jews and heathens. They are all equally the desire of his heart.

Now there is but one possible way for man to attain this salvation or life of God in the soul. There is not one for the Jew, another for a Christian, and a third for the heathen. No; God is one, human nature is one, salvation is one, and the way to it is one; and that is, the desire of the soul turned to God. When this desire is alive and breaks forth in any creature under Heaven, then the lost sheep is found and the shepherd has it upon his shoulders. Through this desire the poor Prodigal Son leaves his husks and swine and hastens to his father. It is because of this desire that the father sees the son while yet afar off, that he runs out to meet him, falls on his neck and kisses him. No sooner is this desire arisen and in motion towards God, but the operation of God's Spirit answers to it, cherishes and welcomes its first beginnings – signified by the father's seeing and having compassion on his son whilst yet afar off, that is, in the first beginnings of his desire. Thus this desire does all, it brings the soul to God and God into the soul, it unites with God, it co-operates with God, and is one life with God. Suppose this desire to be awakened and fixed upon God, though in souls that never heard either of the Law or Gospel, and then the divine life or operation of God enters into them, and the new birth in Christ is formed in those who never heard of his name. And these are they 'that shall come from the East, and from the West, and sit down with Abraham and Isaac in the Kingdom of God'.

Not everyone who says to me, 'Lord, Lord' will enter the kingdom of Heaven, but only those who do the will of my heavenly Father.
Matthew 7.21.

Religion is within

The place of religion is within; its work and effect is within; its glory, its life, its perfection is all within; it is merely and solely the raising of a new life, a new love, and a new birth in the inner spirit of our hearts.

Oh, sir! would you know the blessing of all blessings; it is this God of Love dwelling in your soul, and killing every root of bitterness that is the pain and torment of every earthly, selfish love.

He who lives in the shelter of the Most High, who lodges under the shadow of the Almighty, says of the Lord, 'He is my refuge and fortress, my God in whom I put my trust'. Psalm 91.1–2.

The Holy Trinity

When man was created in his original perfection, the Holy Trinity was his creator. When man was fallen and had lost his first divine life, then there began a new language of a redeeming religion. Father, Son and Holy Ghost were now to be considered, not as creating every man as they created the first man, but as differently concerned in raising the fallen race of mankind to that first likeness of the Holy Trinity, in which their first father was created. So the Scriptures speak of the Father as drawing and calling men, because the desire which is from the Father's nature must be the first mover ... The Son of God is the regenerator or raiser of a new birth in us, because he enters a second time into the life of the soul in order that his own nature and likeness may be again generated in it, and that he may be that to the soul in its state which he is to the Father in the Deity. The Holy Ghost is represented as the sanctifier or finisher of the divine life restored in us because, as in the Deity, the Holy Ghost proceeds from the Father and the Son as the amiable blessed finisher of the triune life of God. So the fallen nature of man cannot be raised out of its unholy state, till the Holy Spirit rises up in it.

The doctrine of the Holy Trinity is thus wholly practical; it shows us our high origin, the greatness of our fall, and the deep and profound operation of the Triune God in the recovery of the divine life in our souls. For as everything that is in us, whether it be heaven or hell, rises up and is generated in us by the will-spirit of our souls, so this mystery of a triune Deity manifesting itself as a Father creating, a Son or Word regenerating, and a Holy Spirit sanctifying us, is to show us from what a height and depth we are fallen. It is to excite such a prayer and faith, such a hungering and thirsting after this triune fountain of all good, as may help to generate and bring forth in us that first image of the Holy Trinity in which we were created.

I have told you these things while I am still with you; but the advocate, the Holy Spirit whom the Father will send in my name, will teach you everything and remind you of all that I have told you. John 14.25–6.

Heaven ...

Heaven is as near to our souls as this world is to our bodies; and we are created, we are redeemed, to have our conversation in it. God, the only good of all intelligent natures, is not an absent or distant God, but is more present in and to our souls than our own bodies. We are strangers to Heaven and without God in the world for this reason only; because we are void of that spirit of prayer which alone can and never fails to unite us with the One only Good, and to open Heaven and the Kingdom of God within us ...

We are all of us by birth the offspring of God – more nearly related to him than we are to one another – for in him we live, and move, and have our being. The first man that was brought forth from God had the breath and spirit of Father, Son, and Holy Ghost breathed into him, and so he became a living soul. Thus was our first father born of God, descended from him, and stood in Paradise in the image and likeness of God. He was the image and likeness of God, not with any regard to his outward shape or form, for no shape has any likeness to God; but he was in the image and likeness of God because the Holy Trinity had breathed their own nature and Spirit into him.

As the Deity, Father, Son and Holy Spirit are always in heaven and make heaven to be everywhere, so this Spirit, breathed by them into man, brought heaven into man along with it; and so man was in heaven as well as on earth; that is, in paradise, which signifies an heavenly state or birth of life.

Where can I escape from your spirit, where can I flee from your presence? If I climb up to heaven, you are there; if I make my bed in Sheol, you are there. Psalm 139.7–8.

... and Hell

Ask now what hell is? It is nature destitute of the Light and Spirit of God and full only of its own darkness; nothing else can make it to be hell. Ask what heaven is? It is nature quickened, enlightened, blessed, and glorified by the Light and Spirit of God dwelling in it .

Heaven and hell have each of them their foundation within us. They come not into us from without, but spring up in us according as our will and heart is turned either to the Light of God or the kingdom of darkness.

The will is that which has all power. It unites all that is united in heaven or on earth, it divides and separates all that is divided in nature. It makes heaven, and it makes hell; for there is no hell but where the will of the creature is turned from God, nor any heaven but where the will of the creature works with God.

I know of no hell, either here or hereafter, but the power and working of anger, nor any heaven but where the God of Love is all in all, and the working life of all.

They are not in hell because Father, Son and Holy Ghost are angry with them, and so cast them into a punishment which their anger had contrived for them. They are in anger and darkness because they have done to the Light which infinitely flows out from God, as that man does to the light of the sun, who puts out his own eyes.

Be sure to bear in mind this day that the Lord is God in heaven above and on earth below; there is none other. Deuteronomy 4.39.

A spark of the Deity

Here you may see the sure ground of the absolute impossibility of the annihilation of the soul. Its essences never began to be, and, therefore, can never cease to be. They had an eternal reality before they became a distinct soul, and, therefore, they must have the same eternal reality in it. It was the eternal Breath of God before it came into man, and therefore the eternity of God must be inseparable from it. It is no more a property of the Divine Omnipotence to be able to annihilate a soul than to be able to make an eternal truth become a fiction of yesterday.

Every motion, stirring, imagination and thought of your mind, whether in fancying, fearing or loving everlasting life, is the same infallible proof that you stand in the midst of eternity, are an offspring and inhabitant of it, and must be for ever inseparable from it.

Were not the essences of your soul as old, as unbeginning, as unchangeable, as everlasting as truth itself, truth would be at the same distance from you, as absolutely unfit for you, as utterly unable to have any communion with you, as to be the food of a worm.

Your mind could receive no truth, feel no delight and satisfaction in the certainty, beauty and harmony of it, unless truth and the mind stood both in the same place, had one and the same unchangeable nature – unbeginning, original. If there will come a time when thought itself shall cease, when all the relations and connections of truth shall be untied, then, but not till then, shall the knot or band of your soul's life be unloosed.

It is a spark of the Deity, and, therefore, has the unbeginning, unending life of God in it. It knows nothing of youth or age, because it is born eternal. It is a life that must burn for ever, either as a flame of light and love in the glory of the divine majesty, or as a miserable firebrand in that God which is a consuming fire.

The souls of the just are in God's hand; no torment will touch them.
Wisdom 3.1.

The cure of every evil

Whether you consider perfection or happiness, it is all included in the Spirit of Love. The infinitely perfect and happy God is mere Love, an unchanged Will to all Goodness. Every creature must be corrupt and unhappy, so far as it is led by any other will than the one Will to all Goodness. No one can be a child of God except as the goodness of God is in it. For as God is an Immutable Will to all Goodness, so the Divine Will can unite or work with no creaturely will but that which wills with him only that which is good.

All contrivances of holiness, all forms of religious piety, signify nothing, without this will to all goodness. For as the Will to all Goodness is the whole nature of God, so it must be the whole nature of every service or religion that can be acceptable to him. Nothing serves God, or worships and adores him, but that which wills and works with him. Everything that follows an own will, forsakes the one Will to all Goodness, and whilst it does so has no capacity for the Light and Spirit of God. As it was his Will to all Goodness that brought forth angels and the spirits of men, so he can will nothing in their existence but that they should live and work and manifest the same Spirit of Love and goodness which brought them into being.

There can be no peace for the soul of man, but in the purity and perfection of its first created nature. Nor can it have purity and perfection in any other way than in and by the Spirit of Love. For as Love is the God that created all things, so Love is the Purity, the Perfection, and Blessing of all created things; and nothing can live in God but as it lives in Love. Look at every vice, pain, and disorder in human nature; it is the creature turned from the universality of Love to some self-seeking or self-will in created things. So that love alone is, and only can be, the cure of every evil. He that lives in the purity of love is risen out of the power of evil into the freedom of the one Spirit of Heaven.

Consider how great is the love which the Father has bestowed on us in calling us his children! For that is what we are. 1 John 3.1.

All are called to be holy

Though all are not called to be prophets or apostles, yet all are called to be holy, as he who has called them is holy, to be perfect as their heavenly Father is perfect, to be like-minded with Christ, to will only as God wills, to do all to his honour and glory, to renounce the spirit of this world, to have their conversation in heaven, to set their affections on things above, to love God with all their heart, soul and spirit, and their neighbour as themselves.

Behold a work as great, as divine and supernatural, as that of a prophet and an apostle.

Dear friends, we are now God's children; what we shall be has not yet been disclosed, but we know that when Christ appears we shall be like him, because we shall see him as he is. 1 John 3.2.

True Christianity

The apostles were new men, entered into a new kingdom come down from heaven, enlightened with new light, inflamed with new love, and preached not any absent or distant thing, but Jesus Christ, as the wisdom and power of God, felt and found within them, and as a power of God ready to be communicated in the same manner, as a new birth from above, to all that would repent and believe in him. It was to this change of nature, of life, and spirit, to this certain immediate deliverance from the power of sin, to be possessed and governed by gifts and graces of an heavenly life, that men were then called to, as true Christianity. And the preachers of it bore witness, not to a thing that they had heard, but to a power of salvation, a renewal of nature, a birth of heaven, a sanctification of spirit, which they themselves had received. Gospel Christianity then stood upon its own true ground; it appeared to be what it was. And what was it? Why, it was an awakened divine life set up amongst men; itself was its own proof; it appealed to its proper judge, to the heart and conscience of man, which was alone capable of being touched with these offers of a new life.

For anyone united to Christ, there is a new creation: the old order has gone; a new order has already begun. 2 Corinthians 5.17.

'I stand at the door and knock'

Neither Christ nor his benefits and blessings have the nature of things done, or gone and past, but are always present, always in being, always doing and never done.

'Jesus Christ, the same yesterday, today and for ever,' always was, now is, and ever will be present as the Saviour of the world. He is the Alpha and Omega, the beginning and the end, and therefore equally present in and through all from the beginning to the end.

'Behold,' says he, 'I stand at the door and knock; if any man hear my voice and open the door, I will come in to him and will sup with him.' Thus he stood at the door of Adam's heart as near as he stood to the apostles'; and thus he stands, and will stand, knocking at the door of every man's heart until time shall be no more.

I am the vine; you are the branches. Anyone who dwells in me, as I dwell in him, bears much fruit; apart from me you can do nothing.
John 15.5.

Endnotes

Preface

1. William Law, *A Serious Call to a Devout and Holy Life*, vol. 4, p. 158.
2. Ibid., p. 228.

Part One
Loving the Hell Out of Us

1. 'This Be The Verse' in Philip Larkin, *Collected Poems* (Faber and Faber, London, 1988), p. 180. Stanza #1.
2. Mark 12.29–31.
3. Thomas Keating, *Invitation to Love* (Element, 1992).
4. Isabel Menzies, *The Functioning of Social Systems as a Defence Against Anxiety* (Tavistock Institute, 1970).
5. 1 John 4.18.
6. Mark 10.17–22.
7. John 20.17.
8. John 18.25–7.
9. See p. 48 of this book.
10. Proverbs 23.7 Authorised Version.
11. See p. 45 of this book.
12. See p. 60 of this book.
13. Ibid.
14. See p. 63 of this book.
15. See Mary Margaret Funk, *A Mind at Peace* (Lion, 1999 – first published as *Thoughts Matter* by Continuum in the USA in 1998).
16. A thought from Mrs Pat Travis.
17. See p. 101 of this book.
18. The titles of William Law's three best-known mystical books are *The*

Spirit of Prayer, The Way to Divine Knowledge and *The Spirit of Love,* and they are cleverly combined in the Collect for William Law Day, which is April 10th in the Anglican Communion.

19. Matthew 21.1–11.
20. See p. 33 of this book.
21. Matthew 19.29.
22. 2 Corinthians 12.10.
23. A saying of the Revd Dr James (Jim) Gibbs.
24. See p. 74 of this book.
25. Archbishop Robert Runcie at the marriage of HRH Prince Charles and Diana, Princess of Wales.
26. See P. Trower, A. Casey, and W. Dryden, *Cognitive-Behavioural Counselling in Action* (Sage, 1988).
27. Psalm 46.10, A.V.
28. See p. 129 of this book.
29. See John 4.34.

William Law's place in Christian Mysticism

1. E.g., Proverbs 8.15, Luke 20.25, John 19.1–2 and Romans 13.1–7.
2. Matthew 5.48.
3. Luke 15.11–32.
4. Luke 18.9–14.
5. John 7.53–8.11. All from the Revised English Bible.
6. R. Llewelyn and E. Moss (ed.), *Fire from a Flint, Daily Readings with William Law* (Darton, Longman and Todd, 1986), p. xii.
7. A. Keith Walker, *William Law – His Life and Work* (SPCK, 1973).
8. Llewelyn and Moss, op. cit., p. xviii.
9. E.g., 2 Peter 2.4.
10. John Donne, *Devotions upon Emergent Occasions.*
11. A loadstone is a magnet.
12. Llewelyn and Moss, op cit., pp. xxii–xxiii

References

Part Two
God and Humanity

Page
33.   Spirit of Love, vol. 8, pp. 3–4.
34.   Appeal to Doubt, vol. 6, p. 128.
35.   Spirit of Prayer, vol. 7, pp. 14–15.
36.   Ibid., p. 15.
37.   Spirit of Love, vol. 8, p. 108.
38.   Spirit of Prayer, vol. 7, p. 109.
39.   Ibid. p. 108.
40.   Ibid. pp. 108–9.
41.   Christian Regeneration, vol. 5, p. 156.
42.   Spirit of Love, vol. 8, pp. 108–9.
43.   Appeal to Doubt, vol. 6, p. 117.
44.   Divine Knowledge, vol. 7, p. 149.
45.   Spirit of Prayer, vol. 7, p. 4.
46.   Spirit of Love, vol. 8, pp. 30–1.
47.   Address to Clergy, vol. 9, p. 23.
48.   Spirit of Love, vol. 8, p. 8.
49.   Spirit of Prayer, vol. 7, pp. 65–6.
50.   Christian Regeneration, vol. 5, pp. 140–1.
52.   Spirit of Prayer, vol. 7, p. 47.
53.   Ibid., pp. 28–9.
54.   Ibid., p. 29.

Hubris and Prayer

57.   Dr Trapp, vol. 6, pp. 32–3.
58.   Appeal to Doubt, vol. 6, p. 61.

59. Divine Knowledge, vol. 7, pp. 211–2.
60. Dr Trapp, vol. 6, p. 33.
61. Spirit of Prayer, vol. 7, pp. 65, 105.
62. Christian Regeneration, vol. 5, p. 179.
63. Letters, vol. 9, pp. 149–50, 152.
64. Address to Clergy, vol. 9, p. 9.
65. Ibid., pp. 20, 52, 54.
67. Spirit of Prayer, vol. 7, p. 74.
68. Ibid., p. 101.
69. Address to Clergy, vol. 9, p. 56.
70. Spirit of Prayer, vol. 7, pp. 98–9.
71. Spirit of Love, vol. 8, pp. 115–6.
72. Address to Clergy, vol. 9, pp. 54–6.
73. Spirit of Love, vol. 8, p. 130.
74. Christian Regeneration, vol. 5, pp. 153–4.
75. Spirit of Prayer, vol. 7, p. 27.
76. Ibid., pp. 27–8.
77. Appeal to Doubt, vol. 6, pp. 80–2.
78. Spirit of Prayer, vol. 7, pp. 25–6.
79. Christian Regeneration, vol. 5, p. 152.
80. Ibid., pp. 153–4.
81. Spirit of Prayer, vol. 7, p. 107.
82. Letters, vol. 9, pp. 178–9.
83. Appeal to Doubt, vol. 6, p. 94, Fire from a Flint, p. 17.
84. Spirit of Love, vol. 8, pp. 122, 125–6.
85. Ibid., pp. 126–7.
86. Christian Regeneration, vol. 5, pp. 156–7.
87. Appeal to Doubt, vol. 6, pp. 139–40.
88. Spirit of Love, vol. 8, pp. 55–6.
89. Ibid., p. 85.
90. Spirit of Prayer, vol. 7, pp. 24, 35.
91. Ibid., pp. 22–3.
92. Dr Trapp, vol. 6, p. 46.
93. Demonstration, vol. 5, pp. 92–3, 117.
94. Spirit of Prayer, vol. 7, p. 26.
95. Ibid., pp. 104–5.
96. Ibid., p. 37.
97. Ibid., p. 43.
98. Ibid., pp. 121–2.
99. Ibid., pp. 58–9.

100.   Ibid., pp. 126–7.
101.   Ibid., pp. 118–19.
102.   Appeal to Doubt, vol. 6, pp. 134–5.
103.   Spirit of Prayer, vol. 7, p. 136.
104.   Ibid., pp. 132–4.
105.   Ibid., pp. 130–1.
106.   Ibid., pp. 131–3.
107.   Ibid., vol. 8, p. 5; vol. 7, p. 48.

Practice and Salvation

111.   Spirit of Prayer, vol. 7, p. 35.
112.   Spirit of Love, vol. 8, p. 52.
113.   Ibid., pp. 74–5.
114.   Ibid., pp. 100–1.
115.   Letters, vol. 9, p. 174.
116.   Divine Knowledge, vol. 7, p. 197.
117.   Letters, vol. 9, pp. 180–1, 183.
118.   Letters, vol. 9, pp.187–8.
119.   Spirit of Love, vol. 8, pp. 4–5.
120.   Manuscript quoted by Hobhouse.
121.   Address to the Clergy, vol. 9, pp. 54–5.
123.   Divine Knowledge, vol. 7, pp. 250–1.
124.   Ibid., pp. 179–80.
125.   Letters, vol. 9, p. 120.
126.   Divine Knowledge, vol. 7, pp. 232–4.
127.   Ibid., p. 234.
128.   Spirit of Prayer, vol. 7, pp. 31–2.
129.   Ibid., pp. 45–6.
130.   Ibid., vol. 7, p. 110, vol. 8, p. 4.
131.   Appeal to Doubt, vol. 6, pp. 77–8, 82–3.
133.   Spirit of Prayer, vol. 7, p. 4.
134.   Ibid., vol. 7, pp. 114, 133, 217; vol. 8, p. 38,
        vol. 6, p.129.
135.   Appeal to Doubt, vol. 6, pp. 64–5.
136.   Spirit of Love, vol. 8, pp. 5–6.
138.   Ibid., pp. 45–6.
139.   Divine Knowledge, vol. 7, pp. 181–2.
140.   Demonstration, vol. 5, p. 61.

Select Bibliography
of William Law

Works of the Reverend William Law M.A.
Edition: G. Moreton, London 1892–3.

Volume IV
A Serious Call to a Devout and Holy Life, 1729.

Volumes V-IX contain Law's mystical writings.

Volume V
A Demonstration of the Errors of 'A Plain Account of the Nature and End of the Sacrament of the Lord's Supper', 1737.
The Grounds and Reasons of Christian Regeneration, 1739.

Volume VI
An Answer to Dr. Trapp's Discourse, 1740.
An Appeal to All that Doubt the Truths of the Gospel, 1740.
Some Animadversions on Dr. Trapp's Reply, 1740.

Volume VII
The Spirit of Prayer, First Part 1749; Second Part 1750.
The Way to Divine Knowledge, 1752.

Volume VIII
The Spirit of Love, First Part 1752; Second Part 1754.
A Short Confutation of Dr. Warburton's Defence, 1752.
Of Justification by Faith and Works, 1760.

Volume IX
An Address to the Clergy, 1761.
A Collection of Letters, 1760.
Letters to a Lady inclined to Rome, 1779.

Llewelyn, Robert and Moss, Edward (ed.), *Fire from a Flint: Daily Readings with William Law* (Templegate, 1987). All the passages are taken from the later, mystical works of William Law. The excellent introductory essay is a fine complement to Walker's biographical study. It is only seventeen pages long and contains many important insights.

Spencer, Sidney (ed.), *The Spirit of Prayer – The Spirit of Love* (James Clarke, 1969). This is a good edition of Law's two great mystical works with useful footnotes.

Spencer, Sidney, *Mysticism in World Religion* (Penguin Books, 1963, Allen & Unwin; J. S. Barnes, New Jersey, 1966).

Hobhouse, Stephen, *William Law and Eighteenth Century Quakerism* (George Allen & Unwin Ltd., 1927).

Hobhouse, Stephen (ed.), *Selected Mystical Writings of William Law* (C. W. Daniel Co. Ltd., 1938).

Hobhouse, Stephen, 'Fides et Ratio, the Book which introduced Jacob Boehme to William Law' (*Journal of Theological Studies*, October, 1936, vol. XXXVII, no. 148).

Inge, W. Ralph, *Christian Mysticism* (Methuen, 1899).

Inge, W. Ralph, *Studies of English Mystics* (Murray, 1906).

Overton, J. H., *Wm. Law, non-Juror and Mystic* (London, 1881).

Spurgeon, Caroline F. E., 'William Law and the Mystics,' in *Cambridge History of English Literature,* ed. Ward, A. W. and Waller, A. R., vol. 9 (Cambridge, 1913).

Talon, Henri, *William Law, A Study in Literary Craftsmanship* (Rockliff of London, 1948). Contains a useful bibliography.

Tighe, Richard, *A Short Account of the Life and Writings of the Late Reverend William Law* (London, 1813).

Walker, A. Keith, *William Law – his Life & Work* (SPCK, 1973).

Walton, C., *Notes and Materials for an adequate Biography of William Law* (London, 1856).

Whyte, Alexander, *Characters and Characteristics of William Law, Nonjuror and Mystic* (Hodder & Stoughton, 1893).

The Churches' Fellowship
for Psychical and Spiritual Studies

The CFPSS exists to promote the study of psychical and religious experience within a Christian context. Founded in 1953 by a group of clergy and laymen on an ecumenical basis, it continues to serve the churches and its individual members who come from many and varied backgrounds. Some have sought help from the Fellowship's extensive knowledge, at significant points in life where there may have been spontaneous gifts of the Spirit, the pain of bereavement or simply a vocation to a spiritual life through psychic encounter. Many bring a wisdom and depth of vision to enrich the understanding of others.

The Fellowship takes a positive view of psychic sensitivity which many people experience quite naturally in their lives, perhaps through an unsought telepathic communication. Some seem to have a greater awareness of this dimension than others and in some it is more refined. There is a gentle call on members to relate this to a fuller Christian life in which the psychic may find consecration.

There are two classes of membership: full and associate. Those eligible for full membership must be practising members of Churches which are members of or affiliated to the World Council of Churches, or must themselves acknowledge Jesus Christ as Lord and Saviour of the World. Associate members, who cannot vote or hold office, need no such qualifications and may be elected if the Council of the Fellowship so determines.

Full and associate members receive the *Christian Parapsychologist* and the *Quarterly Review* four times a year. There is a library, and study material, cassettes and video tapes, books and booklets are available. A fuller prospectus together with lists of the above are available from:

**The General Secretary, CFPSS,
South Road, North Somercotes,
Louth, Lincolnshire LN11 7PT**

Telephone and Fax: 01507 358845
e-mail: gensec@cfpss.freeserve.co.uk